The
Good
Granny
Guide

The Good Granny Guide

Jane Fearnley-Whittingstall

Illustrations by Alex Fox

This paperback edition first published in 2006 by
Short Books
3A Exmouth House
Pine Street
London EC1R 0JH

11

A CIP catalogue record for this book
is available from the British Library.

Illustration Copyright ©
Alex Fox

ISBN 1-904977-70-7

Printed in Great Britain by
CPI Bookmarque, Croydon, CR0 4TD

JACKET ILLUSTRATION: ALEX FOX

**Every effort has been made to contact copyright holders for use of
material in this book, and the publishers would welcome any errors or
omissions being brought to their attention.**

Jane Fearnley-Whittingstall has written many
books on plants and gardening, including
Gardening Made Easy and The Imperial Flower.
The grandmother of five, and mother of
TV chef Hugh, she lives with her husband
in Gloucestershire

For my grandchildren:
Chloe, Max, Oscar, Guy and Freddie

Dear Granny and
Grandpa

Thankyou
fro looking after me.

CONTENTS

INTRODUCTION

'Don't have children, only grandchildren.'

Gore Vidal

The surge of joy when I held my first grandchild in my arms took me completely by surprise, in spite of the fact that I had been looking forward to that moment with almost unbearable excitement for nearly nine months. The relationship between grandparents and grandchildren comes at a time when, for many of us, other relationships and friendships have settled into a customary and predictable pattern. It may turn out to be one of the most fulfilling and mutually rewarding of our lives.

It is a relationship that, until recently, has only been available to a minority. For centuries the average expectation of life was so short that relatively few men and women lived to see their grandchildren grow up. Even in our grandparents' generation, the symptoms of age appeared early, and if we remember them at all, we tend to remember them as old and somewhat remote. But things have changed. Today in Britain there are 16.5 million grandparents, and most of us are very different from the stereotypical grey-haired person dressed in black. One in every two people is a grandparent by the age of 54. Furthermore, we all expect to live much longer and remain healthier than grandparents did in the past.

This change has come about so fast that it is, perhaps, not surprising there is little advice available for grandparents who are keen to fulfil their role in the best possible way. When grandmothers meet, they love to discuss their grandchildren, to compare notes and to boast a little. They also talk about the lack of useful information. When my first grandchild was born, eager to do everything right, I looked through the index of half a dozen of the most popular childcare manuals. 'Grandparents' only got a mention in one book; it gave just two out of 600 pages to the relationship between parents and 'in-laws', which it treated more as a problem to be wary of than as something positive. 'There are so many books written for parents,' we grandmothers say to each other, 'why are there none for grandparents?' Well, there is one now.

You may wonder what makes me think I am qualified to write it. I am not a childcare expert or a psychologist. But I am an enthusiastic, loving and closely involved grandmother of four children. I have talked to or corresponded with more than 200 grandmothers and 50 mothers, and the internet has given me access to many more. All the advice offered in this book comes from the horse's mouth. It is based on the direct, real-life experience of grandmothers and their families, backed up, where necessary, by technical expertise taken from the childcare books our children use. And just to keep a balance between the generations, I have kept by me *Dr Spock's Baby and Child Care*. I no longer have my well-thumbed copy from the 1960s, and had to go out and buy a new one. The latest edition runs to 800 pages, an indication of how daunting the task of bringing up children has become for the new generation.

The task seems even more daunting when both parents are working. Nearly half of all mothers are at work, and the inevitable result is that they are able to spend less time with their children than they would like. This is where we come in – time, that precious commodity, is the best gift we can offer our grandchildren. In the modern, high-tech world in which everything moves so fast, grannies are there to apply the brakes.

In my discussions with grandparents and parents two phrases came up again and again. One was 'unconditional love'; the other was 'hands-on'. The unconditional love flows in both directions, and is a never-ending source of wonder and joy. We expect and anticipate our own love for our grandchildren, but *their* love for *us* comes as a delightful surprise. You do not have to work for it, it simply flows unbidden. It does flourish all the more, however, if given fertile ground in which to grow, and that is where 'hands-on' becomes so important. The more you do for and with your grandchildren, the closer you become.

My book is designed to help you achieve this closeness. Even the best grannies sometimes encounter difficulties, and I hope *The Good Granny Guide* will help you deal with them. It contains tips on how to gain a grandchild's confidence and trust, how to resolve such problems as jealousy, homesickness and temper tantrums, and how to build good relationships with the other adults in your grandchildren's lives.

Some of the advice offered may seem blindingly obvious. You will forgive this if you have ever found yourself opening a cupboard and then forgetting what you went to fetch, or entering a room and pausing on the threshold to try and recall why you are there. These things happen to grannies.

Granny *and* Grandpa

> *Oh we sailed on the sloop John B*
> *My grandfather and me.*
> *Around Nassau town we did roam,*
> *Drinking all night*
> *We got into a fight…*

> (Lyric: The Beach Boys)

Some people have asked why this book is not for grandfathers as well as grandmothers. The answer is, in many ways it is. It is called *The Good Granny Guide* because I am a granny and most of my research was carried out among grannies. But grandfathers are just as important, and they are certainly more closely involved than they used to be a generation ago.

I remember both my grandfathers as rather remote, forbidding figures. My paternal grandpa did his best to entertain us by screwing his monocle into his eye then dropping it by raising a bushy eyebrow. My maternal grandfather, known as 'Pompa' to his grandchildren, read aloud better than anyone I have come across before or since. He specialised in the Uncle Remus stories about Brer Fox and Brer Rabbit and my brother Peter knew the stories by heart. (Peter had beautiful golden curls which ladies found irresistibly tactile, and on one occasion, when a complete stranger approached to stroke the curls, Peter was heard to say, 'Better not come near me, Brer Fox – I'm *monstrous* full of fleas this morning.')

MUMS SAY:
My dad is retired so he has more free time to spend with his grandchildren than he did with us when we were little.

My dad isn't one to show his feelings, but it is plain to see that he adores his granddaughter. On the day she was born, he went through the village they live in, telling everyone he met and beaming from ear to ear.

I adored Mum's dad and he adored me. We were completely inseparable. He was completely different from my father and never shouted or got cross and had oodles of time to just devote to me.

I think it's really admirable when men who had very traditional lives manage to get involved with their grandchildren, even if it's not cuddling or chatting.

Their grandpa has made for them: a wooden easel; a doll's cot; a toy ironing board; a puppet theatre; a bird

table; a playhouse for the garden; an engine shed, turntable, tunnel and goods yard for their wooden railway...etc. etc.

A GRANDFATHER SAYS:
Being a grandfather is wonderful. I don't like to use the word spiritual but a new atmosphere comes upon you. It's a new kind of achievement, a new feeling about the line going on. (Billy Connolly quoted in Yours magazine).

Above all, I hope this book will be read as a celebration of the special grandparent-grandchild relationship, spanning five generations. It records precious memories of our own grandparents and of our mothers and fathers as grandparents to our children. To these memories we can now add the wonder and delight of our own experiences with our grandchildren, and the sheer happiness they bring us.

PART 1 – **FAMILY MATTERS**

CHAPTER 1 – YOU'RE GOING TO BE A GRANDMOTHER

Nobody decides to become a grandparent, it just happens to you – though the biological clock seems to tick for grannies just as it does for mothers. Indeed women who love babies can become broody for grandchildren even before their own children have grown up. My mother could never pass a pram in the street without looking inside it.

There is nothing you can do to bring your grandchild into the world – dropping hints or nagging will have no effect other than to cause your daughter or daughter-in-law extreme irritation. But eventually the day comes when she announces she is pregnant. And then everything changes, including and *especially* your relationship with your children and their partners.

MUMS SAY:
Telling my mother I was pregnant for the first time was a very special experience. I have never felt so close to her.

Having my own children has brought me much closer to my mum. I can now empathise with her emotions regarding us, and understand more fully the psychological roller coaster of motherhood.

GRANNIES SAY:
That was the only thing I wanted in my life: a grandchild.

From the moment my daughter and her partner moved in together, I thought of little else.

Until now, in spite of the fact that your offspring have left home, you have probably maintained a parent-child relationship, with all that that implies. Such relationships are memorably lampooned in a 'Monty Python' sketch, when John Cleese appears in a pinstripe suit and a bowler hat.

'He's such a clever little boy, aren't you? Coochy-

coochy-coo,' says Terry Jones, playing the part of Cleese's mother, and chucking him under the chin.

His mother's friend (Michael Palin) says, 'Ooh, he's a chirpy little fellow… does he talk? Does he talk, eh?'

'Of course I talk,' Cleese replies petulantly, 'I'm the Minister for Overseas Development.'

As parents we may well continue to treat government ministers and high-flying career women as children until they give birth to the next generation. We go on letting them bring their washing home at weekends, and still feel entitled to lecture them about early nights and healthy diets. But as soon as there is a baby on the way, our children themselves acquire parent status. They have finally grown up, and we must consider our nests well and truly empty. If your children used to defer to you and respect your opinions, don't be surprised if they gradually grow out of the habit, and begin expecting you to defer to them, even in matters of child-rearing – especially in matters of child-rearing.

Grandparents-in-waiting are often surprised and impressed by the wonderful confidence of our children's generation. Our daughters and daughters-in-law seem to think they know much more than we do about pregnancy and babies. The advice we can offer on morning sickness, stretch marks, bootees and baby-grows falls on deaf ears unless it happens to coincide with the latest handbook. Good grannies-to-be save their expertise till they are asked for it, and even then it is best to proceed with caution.

If being made redundant as a parent makes you sad, take comfort. It makes you free to take on a wonderful new role that only you can fill: and what is more, you can write your own script to ensure a star performance.

How things have changed

MUMS SAY:
These days we rely on grandparents more for childcare, because more mothers work – but it used to be like this long ago. Fundamentally things have not changed much – it is an eternal relationship.

My mum is definitely more hands on than my nana was, but because today's grannies are more likely to still be working they can have less time available for their grandchildren.

My mum is more young at heart than I remember my grandparents being.

Mum thinks the eco-friendly washing powder I use is rubbish and it doesn't get the stains out. She's sometimes right but I don't care.

A lot has changed since mum had her own children and some of her ideas are outdated but I know her words of advice come from the heart. After having a child myself I can appreciate all her efforts, and I count my blessings every day for having such a wonderful mother.

My mother has made it clear that her approach was very different from my own co-sleeping, breastfeeding, baby-wearing style of parenting.

GRANNIES SAY:
There are far fewer grandchildren in most families now: I was one of 12 grandchildren on my father's side and one of 17 on my mother's.

We are younger in outlook than our own grandparents were, and still living our own lives.

Grandparents these days are much closer to their grandchildren.

As mothers we handled problems differently, not pandering to every whim but being firm but fair. We were more concerned about table manners and appearance.

Today's parents are over-protective; there is too much 'be careful, mind you don't...' As a result, children are more restricted in independence, although they do travel more widely and are culturally more adventurous.

The role of grandmothers varies in different places and at different times in history. In places where, traditionally, able-bodied women have gathered food or tended crops while the men hunted, grandmothers have always played an important part in bringing up children, contributing to the survival of the species by releasing younger women for labour. In such societies grannies have taken over almost all the mother's tasks except breastfeeding. And even that function has occasionally been performed by a grandmother: cases have been recorded in South Africa of postmenopausal grandmothers suckling their newborn grandchildren and, after a month of persevering, producing enough milk to successfully breastfeed a child for as long as two years.

Traditionally, at all times and in all places, grandmothers have also played a strong teaching role, passing on stories, songs and games, showing their grandchildren the rudiments of cooking by allowing them to stir the pot and lick the bowl, and giving them their own lump of dough to roll out and shape into a gingerbread man.

Even in the western world, in some modern industrial societies, it is still normal for grandmothers to play the key role in bringing the new generation up. In Italy, for example, there is very little provision of organised childcare quite simply because there is no call for it; it is taken for granted that the grandparents will look after the grandchildren.

But in Britain the pattern has changed during our lifetime, and is still changing. Grandparents are no longer likely to be living in the same village or town as their children, as would have been the case a generation ago. Still, thanks to improved transport and increased car ownership, frequent, regular visits are possible for many families.

The major change is that many of us are likely to live longer. In spite of the fact that, on average, women are giving birth later, grandparents are relatively young (in a recent study, one third were found to be under 60). Today's women can expect to live to 84 so we are likely to spend between 25 and 30 years as grandparents, and it will not be unusual for us to have several great-grand-children before our days are numbered.

And, while some women are eager to continue in work well beyond the age at which they become grand-mothers, there are still clearly plenty of grannies who prioritise their time to help with the care of their grand-children. There has been a phenomenal increase in the number of private nurseries to meet the needs of the 70-odd per cent of mothers who now go back to work before their baby's first birthday. But in most families grannies are the preferred carers, and, in spite of their own work commitments, more than a third manage to provide childcare for a staggering three days a week or equivalent time. The true value of unpaid grandparental care in the UK has been calculated at over £1 billion a year – though this figure was based on the insultingly low rate of £2.97 an hour (Future Foundation 2002). Politically, there are moves afoot to recognise the contribution grandparents make to the economy by paying them. I believe if any government offered them such a paltry wage, most grannies would consign it to the nappy bucket.

A new image

Women who are scarcely into middle age when they become grandmothers may not feel ready to embrace the traditional role of a granny. They certainly won't want to *look* like a granny. Queen Victoria, for one, whose first grandchild was born when she was 39, was not above boasting about her youthful appearance. 'I own it seems very funny to me to be a grandmamma,' she wrote to her daughter, 'and so many people tell me they can't believe it!'

Even many grannies more advanced in years take a pride in their youthful appearance and lifestyle and, as much as they love their grandchildren, would prefer not to advertise their granny status to the rest of the world. To them, the words 'Grandma', 'Granny' or 'Nana' conjure up that mythical silver-haired old lady who sits knitting. Modern grannies may prefer their grandchildren to call them by their first name, or by some neutral nickname that does not give the game away. Others have names invented by their grandchildren, which have stuck. My maternal grandparents were known as 'Ginny' and 'Pompa' to their thirteen grandchildren; and my first grandson called me 'Mum' for a while because that is what he heard his mother calling me. I have come across grannies called 'Lally', 'Midge', 'Mim', 'Minda', 'Wah-Wah' and 'Zsa-Zsa' to name but a few.

GRANNIES SAY:
I'm absolutely not going to be called Nana or Grandma or any of that stuff. My grandchildren call me by name, like everyone else.

I don't mind what they call me – I seem to have ended up as Ga-ga!

Much has been written about the dashing lifestyle of the new generation of pensioners, the 'silver surfers'.

They are more likely to be auburn, blonde or brunette than silver-haired, and they might just as well be found waiting for a big wave on a Californian beach, or wind-surfing in the Aegean than surfing the internet. These grannies take up new hobbies and sports for the first time, go on adventure holidays in distant places, or even take a gap year. They take full advantage of the fact that their nest is empty, that they have retired from employment, and are free at last to spend their savings on enjoying life. And surveys have found that, naturally enough, such grannies may be neither available nor willing to babysit. They would rather be abseiling in Brecon, SCUBA-diving in the Seychelles or trekking in Nepal.

'Children don't have a right to feel resentful about their parents not spending time with grandchildren,' Emma Soames, editor of *Saga* magazine, has said in an interview in the *Daily Telegraph*. 'The way older people live and spend their time is changing and it does not include being an unpaid nanny.'

GRANNIES SAY:
We grandmothers are as well educated as our children and our thirst is to get back to using that brain which was put on hold during our child-rearing years. I love my grandchildren to bits, but how I yearn to be free!

Think carefully about what you can reasonably do, and make that offer. Don't be bullied into doing more than you want to, and do what you want to do gracefully and willingly.

MUMS SAY:
There never seems to be a good time to have a heart to heart with my in-laws as they are always about to pop off on a cruise.

My son's grandparents are all around 70 years old and are all much more active than me – swimmers, magistrates, hockey umpires, globe-trotters etc.

When her grandchildren were born, my mother let us know she would not get too involved with them... 'I'm going to live life for myself now.'

However, grandparents who see themselves as unpaid nannies are in a minority. Most grandparents value highly the opportunity to establish a deep and lasting rapport with their grandchildren by talking to them, listening to them and playing with them. They want to make sure their grandchildren have a carefree and happy childhood, and may rejoice in the fact that nature has arranged things in such a way that, by the time their grandchildren come along, even those among them with serious careers are beginning to welcome the opportunity to live their life at a slower pace. Parents may be in a hurry, but grandparents should never be.

A MUM SAYS:
I don't see why any grandparent should feel obliged to spend full days with their grandchildren. My own parents see their grandchildren probably once every couple of months and they only live 40 minutes away. They have full and hectic lives themselves and I wouldn't dream of asking more of them.

GRANNIES SAY:
I am happy to be 'used'. That's what grannies are for.

My grandchildren are my absolute priority. They give me a new lease of life and take the stiffness out of being old.

It is so much easier to be a grandparent than a parent – so easy now to stand back and not get caught up in the 'drama'.

Enjoy your grandchildren. They are a great privilege.

A privilege rather than a chore. For many of the grandmothers I corresponded with, this idea went to the very heart of what grandparenting is all about. It is a point nicely demonstrated by the story of the youngest granny I have met, who was 35 when her first grandchild was born. (In Britain there are more schoolgirl mothers than in any other European country, and if their mothers also gave birth at an early age, it would be possible for them to be grannies at 30 – although that would be very exceptional.)

Youngest Granny's first daughter was born when she was 16 going on 17, and her daughter had her first child at 19. Youngest Granny's father had his first child at 19 and became a great grandfather at 56. For a while, then, till her own grandmother died at the age of 94, Youngest Granny had five generations of the family living. She puts it all down to her farming ancestry on both sides and 'naughty teenager' genes.

The situation was further complicated for Youngest

Granny by her giving birth to her second child at the age of 40, 23 years after her first daughter was born. So her second daughter already had a nephew at birth, and is just a few months younger than her own niece. Youngest Granny says that, although her younger daughter and her granddaughter are the same age, she has a different relationship with each of them, loving them 'in entirely different ways. 'With my grandchildren there is the sense that they are someone else's children and therefore I don't have the same sense of responsibility,' she says. 'I don't have to make decisions regarding their education, discipline, what they eat, etc. Having said that, I do worship the ground they walk on!'

So a child's grandparents are not just two spare sets of parents: understudies, waiting in the wings for their big moment when the parents slip on a banana skin. Good grandparents may be prepared to do everything a parent does and more, but they should never forget that the children are not their own. That old cliché about grandparents being able to spoil the child rotten, then hand it back to the parents, is, as clichés usually are, often repeated because there is a lot of truth in it. In the end, the parents, not the grandparents, carry responsibility for their child's physical, emotional and moral development.

If you try to hijack responsibility in any of these areas (and there may be times when the parents are so tired and confused that they will be willing accomplices), you are distorting the parent-child relationship, and that can lead to long-term trouble.

The golden rule for grandparents is never to criticise, even obliquely, the way parents bring up their children; you may not agree with it, but it is none of your business. You are not there at all times to witness the on-going implementation of their parental philosophy. What you see is just the tip of the iceberg, and your best course is to watch, listen and try to understand what your children are trying to achieve. With luck your non-interference will be rewarded by recognition of the grandparental right to spoil.

MUMS SAY:

After raising four boys of her own I think my mother-in-law deserves to just enjoy her grandchildren and feed them sponge fingers and ice-cream for tea if she wants to.

I don't want my mum to see looking after her grandchild as a chore, or as work. I want her to have fun with her the way I think only grandparents can.

Choosing your role

Making the decision about what kind of granny you want to be can prove a marvellously liberating experience: a chance to reinvent yourself at will. You may have fond memories of one or both of your grandmothers, or of your mother as grandmother to your children, and taking them as role models will give you a happy sense of continuity. But your personality may be very different from theirs, and it is best not to try and force yourself into a role that is difficult to sustain. It is more realistic to follow your own character and instincts. Does one of the following descriptions fit you?

Just an Old-fashioned Gran

MUMS SAY:
She is a cuddly, warm, homely, curtain-making, frilly tablecloth sort of granny.

My mother-in-law is a first-time grandma and she often offers advice which I listen to; but a lot of it, e.g. picking cradle cap off, or using talcum powder on the baby's bottom, is the opposite of what the professionals now recommend.

When we'd just started toilet training and our son was having a few accidents his gran wanted to smack him!!

My mother was appalled by my 'demand feeding' chaos, and told me so.

The best kind of old-fashioned granny may well look the part; she may be a cuddly shape, have grey hair, wear a cardigan and slippers, and drop off in front of the telly with her knitting in her lap, snoring gently. She is probably shocked by the way her daughter or daughter-in-law brings up her babies, but she will be philosophical about it, and accept that things have changed, without complaining audibly. In time, she will come round to seeing how successful their methods are, and give praise where it is due.

However, there is also a less accommodating kind of old-fashioned granny. She can be quite aggressive, and determined to let parents know that she doesn't hold with new-fangled ways of doing things. She is likely to say annoying things like, 'a good smack/bedtime at 6.30/tapioca pudding never did any of you any harm.'

Interestingly, until recently the Old-fashioned Gran looked doomed to extinction, and yet the latest trend in childcare, advocated by the popular expert Gina Ford, is very much in line with her ideas — except, of course, for the 'good smack'.

The Glam Gran

She descends on the newborn's cradle like a fairy god-mother bearing gifts of designer baby clothes, cashmere wraps and Tiffany teething rings. In the bad old days before disposable nappies, one such glamorous granny arrived in the maternity ward with a present for her daughter-in-law. It was an exquisite satin and lace night-gown and negligée from Fortnum & Mason. All the young mother could see as she gazed at this generous present were £ signs, adding up to rather more than the price of the washing machine she longed for.

The Glam Gran should never try to turn herself into the nappy-changing, nose-wiping type. She won't suc-ceed. Being warm-hearted, she is always keen to take the baby in her arms for a cuddle, but as soon as she detects damp at either end, she passes the parcel. She doesn't really do babies, darling. But she has plenty of other things going for her.

She will come into her own when her grandchildren are

older, helping them paint their toenails with her nail varnish, giving brilliant presents and thinking up wonderful treats.

MUMS SAY:
My mother-in-law is a very 'glam' grandma and everything in her house is either peach or gold. She has a perma tan, at least three holidays a year and a very toxic perfume. She can captivate her grandson for hours with sophisticated chatter.

She is the most unlikely granny. She gets all her clothes from Topshop, New Look and H&M to look young and trendy. She is very glamorous. Usually she pulls it off, but sometimes it is a bit scary!

The Hands-On Granny

She is the Glam Gran's opposite number. She knows by instinct how to get a burp out of a baby, and how to comfort a colicky one. She even quite likes the smell of baby vomit and won't mind if her grandchild messes up her hair and sticks his fingers up her nose. Instead of the cashmere wrap, her offering to the newborn is a hand-knitted matinée jacket with matching bootees and bonnet.

She always has tissues about her person for mopping dribble and wiping noses, and will spend hours on the floor playing with toddlers. Nothing is too much trouble and she will come to the rescue at a moment's notice. Both her daughter and her daughter-in-law often ask for her advice and even act on it, because she really does know all about babies and she gives her advice tactfully.

As her grandchildren get older she will make almost anything for them, training herself, for example, to become a skilful fletcher, making the best ever bows and arrows.

Mums say:

My mum was absolutely great. She adored the children and loved spending time with them be it winding, feeding, bathing, playing, reading, taking them out, etc.

My granny knitted for Britain.

My mother was a splendid grandmother to my children, from coming to stay while I had my babies and coping with everything, to having a teenager to stay for a term while she crammed for university.

The Wise Woman of the Tribe

This granny is in the tradition of Mother Goose, story-teller and guardian of tales, rhymes and songs to be passed from one generation to the next. It was an immensely important role in the days when most people could not read, and today's grandmother has the same important function: to keep the traditional culture alive by singing the songs and telling the stories. She is also the custodian of her family's history. How else would we know about great-uncle Eric who died in a Liverpool hotel after consuming a great deal of oysters and champagne, having backed the winner of the Grand National? Then there was great-aunt Amy, who took to her chaise-longue at the age of 22 when her husband was killed in World War I, and was never seen with her feet on the ground again.

The Wise Woman knows all there is to know about the ancestors, and will pass it on to her grandchildren, naming the names of mustachio-ed gentlemen in faded photographs, and ladies with big hair, and ample bosoms and hips. Katherine Whitehorn, writing in *Saga* magazine, urges us to 'tell them stories about their more colourful aunts, cousins or ancestors; you are the continuity between the generations, and even kids who just regard them as stories will become grown-ups who are interested in their roots.'

A GRANDCHILD SAYS:
Granny told us wonderful stories, and although she

often repeated the same anecdotes without realising it, she was not the sort to bore on interminably.

A GRANNY SAYS:
The new generation are no longer brought up, at least in the home, on foundational stories that introduce the Christian faith which is their heritage. But the values being dinned in are the same at a deep level.

The Wise Woman is also the guardian of lotions and potions. She has a secret store of gripe water, syrup of figs and other traditional remedies for childish ail-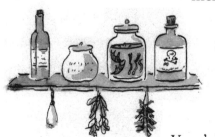ments. My maternal grandmother had a pot of magic ointment to rub on bruises and grazes, known to her grandchildren as 'Mardy Veen'. When I was old enough to read the name on the jar, I found it was called 'Pomade Divine'.

The Wise Woman can always find a dock leaf to rub on a nettle sting. Her extensive repertoire of superstitions and old wives tales includes infallible methods of weather forecasting; she teaches her grandchildren to scan the clouds for enough blue sky to make a pair of sailor's trousers, and to look in the fields to see if the cows are lying down (a sure sign it is going to rain). She sometimes issues rather alarming warnings; for example, 'If you don't stop making hideous faces, the wind will change and your face will be stuck forever.' Our grandmother naughtily assured us that this was what had happened to a very plain great-aunt.

Sporty Granny

She breezes in, straight from the golf course or the tennis court, energy radiating from her. Following the principle that children will have fun if granny is having fun, and granny will have fun if she is doing what she enjoys, Sporty Grannies can be counted on to share their enthusiasm with their grandchildren, and get them off to a good start in their chosen sport or sports.

MUMS SAY:
My grandmother did her exercises on the beach, throwing her legs over her head like the old lady in Babar.

My mother-in-law takes the children on 'Adventure' walks and climbs trees with them.

She goes to the gym, plays golf, is NEVER caught sitting on the sofa eating chocolate and watching TV! She adores her grandchildren and is a wonderful granny.

My mother is unstoppable. She spends hours bowling cricket balls for the children.

Rock'n'roll Granny

She may or may not qualify for her bus pass. It is completely irrelevant, since she makes no concessions to her age or her granny status in the way she dresses and her lifestyle in general. A friend of mine is just such a granny, and made an appearance in the very first *Teletubbies* series.

For this occasion her two granddaughters, Delilah and Cecilia, were filmed 'Packing to stay with granny'. When the little suitcases were packed and ready, children and camera crew waited at the front door for granny to arrive and take them home with her. With a screech of brakes, a brand new scarlet jeep complete with black and white cowhide seats drew up, and out stepped granny, her long legs encased in tight leather trousers, her lipstick the same colour as the jeep.

Daughters and daughters-in-law often despair of Rock'n'roll Granny, complaining about 'the smoking and drinking, the junk food, the late nights,' but they forgive everything because granny and her grandchildren are madly in love with each other. Often a self-confessed bad mother, she makes up for it with the new generation and, as well as providing endless fun, she turns out to be a fund of wise advice.

MUMS SAY:

My mum-in-law smokes like a chimney, drives a 'ute' and a quad bike, hardly eats but is fanatical about decent wine. She loves to be made to laugh. She doesn't seem to have a maternal bone in her body, but loves her grandson to distraction and thinks he is the brightest, most wonderful child that ever walked the planet.

She has just had her eyebrows tattooed on and always travels with her Carmen rollers. She may not have been the best mother but has proved to be an outstanding grandmother. She is completely herself, with a crazy lifestyle and provides huge colour in the children's lives. They adore her.

My mother and my children are involved in a long love affair. I am odd man out.

My mother-in-law drinks like a fish and swears like a trooper. She is the life and soul of ever party and tells great stories about her wild past. I have a soft spot for her and her grandchild simply worships the ground she walks on.

The Granny from Hell

One version of this alarming species of granny was the character immortalised in the 1950s and 60s by the cartoonist Giles. He showed grandma riding a motor-bike, at the head of a posse of Hell's Angels, terrorising the neighbourhood.

The idea was taken up by Monty Python's Flying Circus in a sketch called 'Hell's Grannies'. It showed a gang of old ladies using their handbags to beat up cower ing young men. 'Over these streets hangs a pall of fear...' said the voice-over. A policeman described pension days as the worst – 'They go mad. As soon as they get their hands on their money they blow it all on milk, bread, tea, tins of meat for the cat...'

A young man blames the grannies' hooliganism on addiction: 'Our gran used to be happy until she started on the crochet... Now she can't do without it. Twenty balls of wool a day, sometimes. If she can't have it she gets violent.'

In the past, real life grandmothers were seldom violent but could be frightening. Old age itself can, alas, be unattractive and alarming, and old-fashioned standards of behaviour can be bewildering. One mid-20th-century granny is described by her granddaughter (now herself a granny) as 'formidable: deportment, impeccable table manners and being seen and not heard were what counted. My mother treated her as if she were the Queen and expected us to do the same. We were terrified of her.' Another remembers both her grandmothers as 'horrible, really, and very, very old.' One was neurotic and fretful, the other permanently depressed, and both seemed unreal creatures with whom no true relationship existed.

MUMS SAY:
My father's mother was a dreadful witch of a woman – she was cruel and unkind and we hated her. She lived in Ealing, and used to watch out of the window when I was coming to visit. As soon as she saw me, she would put her head out and order me to walk round the block

50 times before I could come in for tea.

Grandma was quite hairy and a bit scary.

She was a monster autocrat and smelt of stale eau de cologne. She made us recite poetry and never gave us cake for tea.

Nowadays such characters are more likely to be met with in fiction than in the real world. There is a dark side to grannies in folk tales and fairy stories. To the Sakai tribe in Malaya the Queen of Hell is a giantess known as Granny Longbreasts. She washes the souls of the sinful in a cauldron of boiling water.

The granny figure is sometimes unequivocally wicked, like the witch in *Hansel and Gretel*, or the terrifying Russian demon Baba Yaga, with her iron teeth. Baba Yaga lives in a house on chicken's legs and rides round the sky in a mortar, beating the ground with a pestle and sweeping away her tracks with a birch broom. As for our well-loved fairy tale, *Little Red Riding Hood*, in which the gentle, harmless granny metamorphoses into the wicked wolf, what can one say? These stories do grannies no favours at all.

Mad Granny

'You've got mad hair this morning, Granny Jane'
Oscar

Eccentricity is not usually considered desirable in a parent, but is quite acceptable in a grandparent. I recently saw a seven-year-old boy announce to a television interviewer, 'My granddad is absolutely bonkers,' and it was said with real pride.

'Bonkers' would also have been an apt description of Diana Holman-Hunt's paternal grandmother, described in Diana's funny and touching book, *My Grandmothers and I*. The widow of the pre-Raphaelite painter Holman Hunt, her grandmother was known simply as 'Grand', to Diana, and lived in solitary squalor in a large, cold house near Holland Park.

The house was stuffed full of pictures, furniture and *objets*, from Italian Renaissance Old Master paintings and stage props worn by Holman Hunt's models, to a thunderbolt found on the South Downs by Edward Lear and a bundle of Lord Kitchener's letters.

Grand greatly embarrassed Diana by making her go to a party bare-foot, dressed as the Greek goddess Diana in a white robe 'like a choirboy's surplice', bound up with silver ribbons, when she could have worn her red

velvet party frock and black kid shoes with silver buck-
les. '"When we go in," Grand whispered, "hold your head
high and say 'prune'. You must learn to make an entrance
and it makes your mouth look smaller."'

One of Grand's eccentricities was to set up burglar
alarms each night, home-made from bells on tripwires,
and piles of tins.

Supergran

> 'My grandmother... was the most important person to
> me throughout my childhood... She could speak French,
> German and Italian faultlessly, without the slightest
> trace of accent. She knew Shakespeare, Milton and the
> eighteenth century poets intimately. She could repeat
> the signs of the Zodiac and the names of the Nine
> Muses. She had a minute knowledge of English history
> according to the Whig tradition. French, German and
> Italian classics were familiar to her...'
>
> Bertrand Russell, *Autobiography*, 1961

If Bertrand Russell's grandmother represents one kind
of Supergran, Elinor Glyn's (fictional) grandmother's
talents and priorities were rather different. In her novel
Reflections of Ambrosine, Elinor wrote: 'Grandmamma...
has been especially particular about deportment. I have
never been allowed to lean back in my chair or loll on a

sofa, and she has taught me how to go in and out of a room and how to enter a carriage… She has also made me go through all kinds of exercises to insure suppleness, and to move from the hips. And the day she told me she was pleased I shall never forget.

'There are three things she says a woman ought to look: straight as a dart, supple as a snake, and proud as a tiger-lily.'

We may not wish to take either of these extreme examples as our role model, but we still aspire to be Supergran. One purpose of this book is to encourage us in this goal, with a little bit of help from our friends. And it is not such an unattainable one. The truth is that, because of the phenomenon of mutual, unconditional love, our grandchildren in their naive and trusting way, often believe us to be Supergrans without much effort on our part. One of my own proudest moments was when Max, aged five, said out of the blue, 'I think you're fantastic, Granny Jane.'

Here are some testimonials to Supergrans of all kinds, written by their children and grandchildren:

She always assumed we were innocent of any misdemeanours; a refreshing change from our parents who assumed we were guilty until proven otherwise!

She spent lots of time talking to us, asking about school, friends, etc, and just listening: she was always interested in our replies.

Both grandparents were very supportive of us in all our endeavours, always giving subtle encouragement. And I think this helped build our confidence and our belief in ourselves. By comparison, our parents seemed to take our achievements for granted.

I am very close to my grandmother and find her easier to live with than my mother.

Grandparents can get closer to their grandchildren due to the generation gap. It's a case of 'Don't mind the gap,' If you ask me.

My grandmother was an oasis of calm in a very disordered childhood. A gentle but powerful presence.

She puts so much energy into her relationship with the children, and understands them so well. They absolutely adore her.

I simply don't know what I would do without her. When I thank her she just says her mother did it for her.

She is incredibly gentle and patient, and has unreserved love for my children. She is my sounding board on almost everything to do with them.

My mum even now is still my rock. I love her enjoyment of her grandchildren, and the fact that although she is very, very good to them, she doesn't spoil them or let them get away with bad manners, etc.

Here is another thoughtful description of a real-life perfect granny, worth quoting in full: 'My mother has just turned 70. She is glamorous despite hardly ever dressing up; she is fiercely intelligent but never makes anyone feel stupid. She gives both me and her daughter-in-law 'granny weekends' off from childcare every year; she drives 90 minutes every week to appear in my house, do half my housework, all my gardening and cheer up my son. She will happily listen to any of us moaning on about our lives. She has used her retirement to globetrot to Costa Rica, Namibia, Australia, etc. whereas I only really want to go to France. I love her so much and I really hope she emulates her own mother and lives to 97.'

Mothers and daughters tend to have a bit of a head-start in the relationship stakes. When it comes to mothers-in-law and daughters-in-law, though, the picture is rather bleaker. On the whole, during my research, I have found that these two parties do not give each other good references, so it is particularly heart-warming to find this daughter-in-law praising her mother-in-law with such affectionate enthusiasm: 'She's truly wonderful; in her 70s she is still working at various jobs, but will always drop everything if any of her eleven grandchildren or four daughters-in-law need her. Always supportive, never judgmental, she writes to me once a year to thank me for being such a nice wife to her boy and good mother to her youngest grandchild!'

Some of these model grannies who are able to give a great deal of time and energy to their relationship with their grandchildren, might make others with less of either commodity to give feel inadequate by comparison. But there is no need for that. We all give what we are able to give, and it is sometimes a mistake to be over-zealous. I have come across examples of families who resent capable but bossy grannies who try to run their children's lives. One granny's attention was so overwhelming that two of her children virtually broke off relations with her.

Most of our children would prefer us to follow the example of a granny who, according to her daughter-in-law 'never gave advice unless directly asked, never criticised my methods of child-rearing, just played with the children, listened to them and talked to them.' It is *quality*, not quantity of care and attention that is most important.

CHAPTER 2 – RELATIONSHIPS

The arrival of grandchildren does change relationships and it's up to you to make sure the change is for the better. You are not the only adult in your grandchild's life, and the success of your relationship with your grandchildren will depend partly on building up good relationships with the other people around them.

In some families there is a history of negative feelings and behaviour to overcome. Perhaps, since leaving home, your son or daughter has drifted away from you; perhaps you no longer have much in common, or your relationship has always been a stormy one. If so, now is your chance to build a new relationship centred on the children, for whom you both care so much.

On the other hand, problems may have arisen between you and the in-laws; you or they may have been against your children getting together from the start, and a coolness may have developed for this or some similar reason.

It is very natural for some wariness to exist between both you and your fellow in-laws, and you and your daughter-in-law or son-in-law. Most parents start with the suspicion that the chosen partner is not good enough for their darling son or daughter, and they may not even be aware that their feelings show. One mum told me her own mother, 'is quietly critical of my husband's contribution — even though he is a great strength'. Another felt that her mother-in-law was not a warm person, 'perhaps because of the suffering caused by the war'. In both cases the mothers had no idea they gave a negative impression.

Whatever the problem, there is no better time than the birth of a baby to put things right. I can guarantee that you will find that seeing your daughter as a mother for the first time, or your son as a father, is a very happy and emotional moment. And you should let this warmth extend to your daughter-in-law or son-in-law, regardless of how you might have felt towards them in the past. The parents of your grandchild are a couple, inseparable (let's hope), and you will be deeply moved to see how instinctively confident they are together with the baby.

MUMS SAY:
I was a difficult teenager and my relationship with my mother had remained very strained. Having my first baby was a hugely healing, reconciling event for us both.

It brought my father and my husband together – they had been very wary of each other.

I don't think my mother-in-law was a wonderful mother at all, but she is a wonderful Nana and this has helped my husband and her improve their own relationship.

Although she was a disastrous mother she is a brilliant grandmother.

A GRANNY SAYS:
I believe grandchildren bring families together and create a wonderful family unity.

There is no reason why the goodwill engendered by the baby's arrival should not last indefinitely, but it helps if you recognise the need to nurture it a little. This chapter draws your attention to some of the difficulties that can arise, and suggests ways of avoiding them or, if they can't be avoided, limiting the damage.

The other grandparents

Your co-grandparents may be almost complete strangers to you. Perhaps your only meeting before the first grandchild's arrival was the one recorded in the wedding photographs: you and your co-granny's simpers or grimaces half hidden under extravagant hats. But you will probably see more of each other now, as the babies grow into toddlers and the toddlers into schoolchildren.

First, there is the question of what the grandchildren will call you. Until they learn to speak, it is a matter for you both to decide.

A MUM SAYS:
If your grandkids have multiple grandparents, negotiate between yourselves what you want to be called. We have Granny and Grandad on one side, and Grandma and Grandpa on the other. When I was young, mine both insisted on being 'Grandma', so we used to call them 'Fat Grandma' and 'Little Grandma'... I'm sure it could be a LOT worse.

With the names sorted out, you need to address yourself to getting along with your fellow grandparents. You may have very little in common other than your grandchildren, and tact is needed when you talk about them. Any hint of criticism of the way they are brought up may be interpreted as a slur on the other granny's daughter or son or even herself. If no other topic of mutual interest presents itself, try moaning about how 'fings ain't what they used to be'.

Equally, you should never slag off the other granny in front of your grandchildren. To do so upsets and embarrasses them, and challenges their loyalty in an unacceptable way.

In *My Grandmothers and I,* Diana Holman Hunt's Bohemian 'Grand' is furious with her co-granny for suggesting that Diana, on her annual visit, should sleep in a bed rather than on a sofa, be provided with facilities for hanging up her clothes, and have her hair washed. 'It would be most unbecoming for me to criticise your other grandmother in any way and I'm sure she means to be kind but I have always thought her a very worldly woman.'

The 'worldly woman', who was always exquisitely dressed and coiffured, and smelled of violets, had a similarly low opinion of 'Grand'. Diana returned from her visit to be greeted by: 'What a sight! A fright! Your hair — it's just a lifeless frizz... Unbrushed, unwashed, unkempt...' When Diana tried to defend 'Grand' by reporting that she had given her tea at an ABC café one day, Grandmother's response was, 'Stingy old thing! She could at least have taken you to Gunters.'

The key surely to a successful friendship with the in-laws is not to see life as a granny-contest. Apart from anything else, it is a contest you cannot be certain of winning. It's better to accept that your co-grannies have skills that you lack, and to hope your own assets complement theirs.

It didn't take me long, or hurt much, to come to terms with the fact that my co-granny, Granny Joan, can play the piano and sing like an angel. I am the opposite: nobody wants to stand next to me in church. But there is no point in being envious of her talent. Instead, I am pleased she is there to foster any musical gifts that the two little boys inherit from her.

Granny Denise (my other co-granny) is Queen of the Maggots. If that sounds insulting, it is actually high praise. She is expert at baiting fishing lines with anything, no matter now much it wriggles, whereas at the sight of a pullulating tubful of maggots I can't hold on to my breakfast.

Number One Granny

'[A] grandmother must ever be loved and venerated,
particularly one's mother's mother I always think.'
Queen Victoria, 27 June 1859, Letter to her daughter, the
Princess Royal on the birth of her first child.

If your daughter is the baby's mother, that makes you senior granny. This fact, shrewdly observed by Queen Victoria, is confirmed by recent research.

A study carried out by the London School of Hygiene and Tropical Medicine's Centre for Population Studies found that: 'Women are very much the social networkers, with daughters more likely to keep in touch than sons, and grandmothers also working to maintain contact... A grandparent's contact with his or her grandchildren has a lot to do with whether they are the offspring of a son or a daughter. If they are a son's, the grandparents are likely to see less of them than if they are a daughter's.'

The research tells us what we already know by instinct. If you are not the mum's mum, you must yield precedence to your daughter-in-law's mother. She is Number One Granny. All the more reason for you to make sure that you and she get along.

MUMS SAY:
Geography means the two grandmothers don't meet very often. They are very polite but have little in common.

My mother's always very diplomatic but she and my mother-in-law would never be friends.

My mother-in-law was arrogant and tactless and made no effort to get on with my mother.

The children are closer to my mother, but that also means they don't behave so well with her.

The grannies get on very well and have become good friends.

GRANNIES SAY:
I find my son's mother-in-law an absolute nightmare, but I think he does too, so I keep very quiet.

I don't think my mother-in-law was as close to her grandchildren as my mother was. She was more detached. But she is now much respected by my daughter.

The other granny and I are very OK when we meet. I know she thinks the kids should be more disciplined. She said so on Christmas morning: BIG mistake.

The men in your grandchild's life

In the flurry of excitement following the birth of a baby, it is easy for men to get left behind. And, especially if you are Number One Granny, you should make sure that you and your daughter don't make your son-in-law feel like the victim of a female conspiracy. A cosy women's club tends to form around a new baby, centred on the child's needs and performance. Anthony Trollope coined the phrase 'baby worship', an accurate description of the club's rites.

It so happens that this centuries-old, worldwide tradition was strongly reinforced during the childhood of many of today's grandparents, including myself, and of the generation before ours. We were born at the beginning of World War II and our mothers were probably babies or toddlers during World War I. So two generations of fathers were mostly away at the war and missed out on the most formative years of their children. The children spent their early years almost exclusively in female company. In some families the sad truth was that fathers, having endured the trauma of war and missed those important early getting-to-know-you years, were never able to establish the easy, loving relationship with their children that today's fathers can enjoy.

No wonder, when it was time for us to have our own

babies, it seemed natural to join the female conspiracy. Our generation paid lip-service to the modern idea that a baby's father might actually attend the birth, and cracked the odd joke about male chauvinists refusing to do their share of nappy changing, but Dad's Lib, that important spin-off from Women's Lib, had barely begun in our day.

MUMS SAY:
My mum has never, EVER, got over the fact that my husband changes nappies.

My dad always finds me a chair which will be comfortable to feed in. He read up a bit on breastfeeding and embarrassed me by telling his friends when we were eating a curry when my baby was six weeks old that it would be her first curry too!

Even to discuss the father's role seems old-fashioned to our children. They take it completely for granted that he will be closely involved with their babies. To them it is natural for fathers to do everything mothers do except breastfeed. Many fathers bath their children, change their nappies and get up in the night when they cry. Your son or son-in-law is probably just as interested as you are in his offspring's development, and will have firm opinions about the baby's diet and sleep pattern. So make sure, if you embark on discussions with your daughter about the baby's welfare, that you include the baby's father on equal terms.

It is you, the grandmother, who is likely to feel left out when such topics are discussed, and, unless you are expressly asked what you think, you would do well to remain silent, because the principles and methods that you dredge up from the inner recesses of your memory are probably outmoded, or even completely discredited.

Remember, too, that, even if, in the early days, it is her mother whom your daughter wants around for support, the baby has a grandfather too. Don't let him feel left out. Involve him if he wants to be involved, and encourage the children to love him too. His generation are strangers to the hands-on physical care of babies, but it is never too late for them to learn, if they are so inclined.

MUMS SAY:
My dad has made his granddaughter some beautiful wooden toys and I remember when I was little that he would build us go-carts and see-saws and ride on them with us. It will be lovely to see him do the same things with her.

My granddad used to just sit in his chair watching the racing and making roll-ups.

Handling relationships tactfully

When everything is going well, you will be thrilled to discover how useful you can be, especially with the first baby. You may even begin to think you are such a wonderful grandparent they can't manage without you. This is a well-concealed trap. *Don't* fall in.

No matter how close and loving the family is, no matter how useful you are around the house, no matter how much the grandchildren adore you, you are a guest in your son or daughter's house, albeit a special guest, and there is a time when your visit should end. An open-ended arrangement will make everyone uneasy, so agree the length of your visit beforehand and stick to it.

You don't ever want to hear those dreadful whispered words: 'When's she going?' If in doubt, make your visits short. Quit while you're ahead – and leave them wanting more. Apart from anything else, after a few days helping out with a new baby, you will be on your knees and longing for your own bed.

Indeed a particular word of caution should be directed at Number One Grannies in this respect. After the baby is born, and if there is room, your daughter may want you to stay a few days at her house from time to time to help out. You should be aware, however, that the baby's father may be less than thrilled to have his mother-in-law around for days on end. He may be too polite to let you see how he feels, but you are treading on eggshells, so be tactful. See things from his point of view and *don't* lock yourself in the bathroom for a long, relaxing, scented soak just when he wants to shave and shower. *Don't* tell him you have been looking forward all week to watching a classic costume drama on TV just when he is settling down with a can of beer to watch the big match. Do the washing up, leave the bathroom clean and make yourself scarce from time to time so he and your daughter have time together getting to know the baby.

All in all, do your best to be an asset rather than a hindrance. It is sometimes difficult to resist the urge to protest if you think the parents are getting things wrong. After all, grandmothers were mothers not so long ago; they have been there, done that, seen it all. And of course they yearn to pass on their accumulated knowledge and wisdom to the next generation, and to save them from their mistakes.

But Good Grannies do not indicate by so much as a twitching eyebrow that in their day things were done differently and, in their opinion, better. Even if your children ask for your opinion, they will not necessarily welcome it when you give it. They may even laugh at you. Much of the received wisdom has changed since we brought up our own children. So don't confide in your daughter or daughter-in-law that it makes you shudder to see a two-year-old with a dummy in her mouth, or a four-year-old clutching a bottle. How old-fashioned is that, she will be thinking.

Remember, you all have one important thing in common: you want the grandchildren to be happy and healthy, and you want to be trusted to spend lots of time with them. So there is every reason for goodwill to pour out of you. Just in case you need them, though, here are a few tips to oil the wheels:

Do tell the parents as often as you get the chance what wonderful parents they are, and how beautiful, clever, talented and nice the children are. Tell your co-grandparents the same; in general lay on the praise with a trowel. To the parents, their baby boy is always as beautiful as Adonis, their girl lovelier than Helen of Troy. You probably think so too, so don't keep your opinion to yourself, share it.

Do stick to the parents' line on Sex, God and Death. Sooner or later you will have to answer such questions as 'Who is baby Jesus?' and 'What happened to Rex (or the cat, or the rabbit) when he died?' When your grandchild asks you where babies come from, should you launch into a biology lesson or mumble something about the stork or the gooseberry bush? You can't go wrong if you accept the parents' version of matters of life, death and religion, whether or not you approve of it. But you can only do this if you know what their version is. Good Grannies anticipate these awkward moments and check with the parents.

There are some thoughts that grandparents should keep to themselves.

Don't say anything that might imply that your son-in-law/daughter-in-law is really lucky to be married to your daughter/son.

Don't say anything to your daughter or daughter-in-law suggesting that you know more than she does about bringing up children, or that you were a better mother than she is.

MUMS SAY:
I have seen friends made miserable by well-meaning mums who just can't help giving them too much advice and expecting them to bring up their children their way.

Please don't start with the, 'Isn't it time she was out of nappies?' stuff. Constructive advice offered in a loving, supportive way is always welcome. Criticism, implied or overt, is not. Trust that you did your job as parents so well that we will be good parents too.

Please please please don't tell us that we were all dry through the night by 18 months No matter how many times I hear this I DON'T BELIEVE YOU!!!!

That cry from the heart also applies to other variations on the childcare theme. The following phrases are all taboo:

I had you sleeping through the night/weaned/walking/talking before you were...
Goodness, feeding him again?

All babies look the same to me (usually a grandpa remark rather than a granny remark).

We never did that with you.

She's never any trouble when she's with me.

Why don't you...?

Crying exercises their lungs.

I wonder why he isn't smiling/crawling/walking/talking yet...

Pity he has his father's chin/eyes/nose/temper.

Never mind, perhaps the next one will be a boy.

You're *not* going to send them to state schools, are you?

You're not going to send them to private schools, are you?

When are you going to get his hair cut? (Don't even say this when he is 30 years old. *Especially* not when he is 30).

Oh! You've had all my baby's lovely curls cut off.

Don't say to the baby:

It's such a pity I get to see so little of you, isn't it did-dums? [sigh].

Or to your grandchildren:

Let's ask mummy if you can stay up late/watch TV/have sweeties/a puppy for your birthday.

If you have something to say to the parents, say it

direct, not through a fake conversation with your grand-child. It puts the parents in an impossible position. And, *whatever* you do, don't criticise the chosen name. Parents are very sensitive about the names they choose for their children, so if you think the chosen name is ghastly, keep mum. Likewise, do not say, 'Jennifer is a nice name' or, 'Aren't you going to call her by a family name?'

> *Sweetest little fellow*
> *Anybody knows,*
> *Don't know what to call him*
> *But he's mighty like a rose.*

Your granny friends

One of the pleasures of grannyhood is being able to compare notes with your granny friends. A certain etiquette is involved. You don't have to take it too seriously, but playing by the rules will ensure, in the long run, that your friendships not only remain intact, but are enhanced. These are the rules:

> **Don't** show photographs of your grandchildren unless you are asked to. When you are with other grannies, you have to take turns. You need not listen to what the others are saying, but you have to pretend to be interested. Then you can have your turn.

Try not to compare your grandchild's development and achievements with other children's, especially not out loud.

When our own children were growing up we worried constantly if ours were slower than someone else's in learning to smile, crawl, walk, talk, get out of nappies, read or write. We fretted about their chances of winning the egg-and-spoon race or the poetry competition, or making it into the rugby or hockey team. But now we are grandparents we know it is a mistake to make comparisons. None of these things are really important; all children are different, each developing at a different pace. There are plenty of examples. Winston Churchill was famously useless at school. In my own family a boy who did not learn to read until he was eight became in later life a gifted and successful schoolmaster. Perhaps his skill as a teacher was partly due to remembering how difficult learning had been for him at an early age.

So, despite some evidence to the contrary among one's friends, grannies should know better than to boast about their grandchildren's precocious achievements. In the competitive world we live in today, it is the grandparents, with all their experience, who can provide reassurance for over-anxious parents.

Your grandchildren and your pets

There are four new puppies down at the farm,
The jolliest you could see.
The littlest one has a cold wet nose,
And the littlest one's for me.

This chapter is about relationships with people, but it seems the right place to mention pets. If you have a dog or cat, the arrival of your first grandchild on the scene may put their noses out of joint. They will see the baby as an interloping puppy or kitten, a rival for your affection. But if you make a point of introducing the baby to your pets, and let them have a good sniff at her, they will understand that she is a family member, and be reassured. You can reinforce the message that the baby is not there to usurp your pets' position by making rather more fuss of the pets than you normally would.

GRANNIES SAY:
There was a bit of a problem with my Peke as my daughter was terrified he would bite the baby, so for the first year I had to spend a fortune putting the poor dog in kennels when they came. This was bad because the baby never got used to him, but now I think it's OK. I hope so – I'm still nervous, for if he did bite her I'd be excommunicated for ever!! Such a strain!!

My golden retriever adored the baby. He would mount guard beside her and it was almost impossible to shift him. Later he put up with her crawling all over him, and pulling his ears and tail.

I never trusted the cat. She seemed to be looking at the baby with a malevolent eye, patiently waiting for an opportunity to harm him.

99.99% of the time dogs and cats settle down to a perfectly harmonious relationship with babies and toddlers, and it can be touching to see how the animals extend their loyalty and affection to the new generation, proudly watching over the cot or pram. However, once in a while there is a horror story about a dog attacking a child, or a cat smothering a baby in its cot.

To be safe, you must never leave a cat or dog alone in a room with a small child; and children need to be told never to touch an animal while it is sleeping or eating or when it has a bone. Once your grandchildren can walk, it can become more a case of protecting the animals from the children than vice versa. If you have pets but your grandchildren's parents do not, it is at your house that the children can learn to respect animals and be kind to them.

Most cats will do a disappearing act as soon as a grandchild arrives, returning to be fed only after they are in bed. Toddlers do love to chase a cat, though (not out of unkindness but out of curiosity), and, if cornered, the cat will spit and scratch. Luckily, cats are extremely agile, and will usually put themselves well out of the way of trouble before it starts. Dogs are more complicated. A fear of dogs, in particular, is natural in children, especially between the ages of three and five. For safety's sake it is not necessarily a bad thing, and encouraging the child to overcome his fear doesn't usually have much effect. He will get over it in his own good time. But, for every child who is scared of dogs, there is another who is a dog-lover, and considers it a great treat to be allowed to feed granny and grandpa's dog. Backed up by one of the dog's owners, a three or four-year-old can hold the bowl of food, say firmly 'sit' and 'stay' and, when the dog responds, put down the bowl for it to tuck in. As for playing, toddlers, especially boys, are like puppies, and will roll about and wrestle with puppies of the canine kind for ages. Both species learn in this way where the limits are set, but an adult presence is essential to see fair play.

If neither you nor your co-grandparents has any animals, be on your guard. Sooner or later your grandchild will encounter a darling little puppy at a friend's house and yearn for a puppy of his own. If, as they almost certainly will be, his parents are deaf to his pleading, he will try granny, who has always been a soft touch.

A GRANNY SAYS:
I have acquired a dog! I had promised Daphne two years ago I would get one, and had tears from her, 'you never do what you promise', so we went together to a dogs' home and got this puppy – she's awfully sweet but I'm walked off my feet!

The moral of this story is, don't make rash promises, because if you do, you must keep them. The story above does have a happy ending. The granny who, in all her 65 years has never had a dog before, and the puppy and Daphne are all completely infatuated with each other and spend blissful hours in the park together several days a week – Daphne and the dog rushing around wearing themselves out while granny goes at her own pace.

CHAPTER 3 – GETTING TO KNOW YOUR
GRANDCHILDREN

'You can do anything with children if only you play with them.'
Otto von Bismarck

'We are a grandmother.' Margaret Thatcher

'I have been much moved — obsessed is really the word — by the whole thing... here at last, in flesh and blood, is a motive for going on far stronger than any I have encountered during nearly three years of struggle.'
Frances Partridge, *Hanging On*, 1963

'How slowly time goes when one is waiting for a longed-for event,' said Babar, King of the Elephants, to his wife Celeste before the birth of their triplets, Pom, Flora and Alexander. For your family, as for Babar and

Celeste, the time finally comes when the thrill of anticipation tinged with anxiety is over and the baby (or
babies) has (have) arrived. You may have knitted your way
through the last seven or eight months, or just fretted
your way through them. Now being a granny is no longer
a delightful fantasy but a reality. The crumpled, red little
creature you were all waiting for is here.

The first time you hold your first grandchild is unfor-
gettable. You will have imagined the longed-for event,
but the reality, the deep satisfaction, the pride, the gratitude and the sheer love you feel, transcends anything you
imagined. One grandmother used C.S. Lewis's words,
'Surprised by joy' to describe the feeling. What is more,
for most grandparents, that moment of pure joy is only
the first of many. It returns at unexpected moments,
brought on by such trivia as a tiny fist punching the air
during a nappy change, a small hand clutching a squashed
blackberry, a first somersault, an exam passed.

In the early weeks of a baby's life both sets of grandparents are probably falling over themselves and each
other to show their love for the baby. You don't want to
wear out the parents and confuse the baby by all arriving
to pay homage at the same time, so find out when your
co-grandparents are planning to visit. Check, too, on
what presents they want to give, so you don't duplicate.

The parents, you and the co-grandparents will probably already have arranged who gives major items like the crib and the pram. Or perhaps they are handed down from generation to generation. All the babies in our family spent their first months in a cradle dating from the 1960s, trimmed like a lampshade and known, in the words of the song from *Oklahoma*, as 'The Surrey with the fringe on top'.

Tiny babies need no other presents. They certainly don't need another cuddly toy. As one mum complains, 'I have just given two black sacks full of cuddly toys to a jumble sale and we are still knee-deep in the things.' If the itch to give a present is unbearable, ask the parents' advice before you go shopping. They may like the idea of a mobile to hang over the cot or a picture for the nursery wall. Indeed, here is a chance to sneak in one of your own childhood favourites. The two things indelibly printed in my mind from my own childhood nursery go from the sublime to the ridiculous: one is a large reproduction of Botticelli's 'The Mystical Nativity' in an elaborate gilded frame on the wall over the fireplace, the other a bedside rug with Mickey and Minnie Mouse woven into the velvet pile. Both were presents from grandparents. Or you could lay the foundations for your grandchild's library with a few classics.

It is the parents rather than the baby who need thoughtful gifts.

MUMS SAY:
Top three presents to give the parents of a newborn –
1. A homemade hamper of delicious food, wine, bath oil, beauty products, anything else you know they will love.
2. 'Promise' vouchers to be redeemed any time, undertaking to cook, iron, clean or babysit for them.
3. Photograph album.

When my children were born, in the dark ages before disposable nappies were invented, the best present was a nappy service. The dirty nappies were collected from your house and clean ones delivered. Mercifully in most families nappies no longer have to be laundered, but nappy services are still available for families who prefer not to contribute to the 4% of household waste in Britain created by disposable nappies. Apparently it costs the taxpayer £40 million a year to dispose of them. So if your grandchildren's parents want to follow the environmentally sensitive route, the National Association of Nappy Services (www.changeanappy.co.uk) can tell you the nearest local service.

For those who use disposable nappies, an equivalent

present, probably just as much appreciated, is to arrange for a cleaner to come once a week, if the parents don't already have regular help. Rather than hand over the money and expect the tired and harassed young parents to make the arrangements, organise it yourself and announce that is what you have done.

The priority for the parents is to get some sleep. And any way you can help them in this respect will be much appreciated. As soon as the baby is old enough, you can take him or her home with you so the parents have quality time alone together. How often you can help out obviously depends on your circumstances, but anything is good.

Again, communication with the other grandparents is important, to make sure offers of help are evenly spread. At the same time, neither the parents nor you should worry if you sometimes have to say no. It is only too easy, in the thrill of new grandparenthood, to forget you have a life of your own. But try and be available on special dates (write reminders into your diary), for example their wedding anniversary, birthdays and New Year's Eve, in case a last minute request comes. It is invaluable if you can be relied on to take over in a crisis, minor or major.

A MUM SAYS:
My mother-in-law has a very close relationship with them both and will have them if they are too sick for school/childminder but not sick enough to want me! In fact, Nana is better than me when they are poorly as they get loads of pampering and sympathy!

A GRANNY SAYS:
We helped our daughter and son-in-law last year when my grandson badly broke his arm in 2 places, by being there for his younger brother, while they spent time in hospital, and he came to us when mum and dad went back to work.

Another way good grannies can create extra time for the parents is by stocking their freezer with heat-and-serve dishes. They don't have to be homemade, although, if you are the perfect hands-on granny, they will be. Granny Mary, whose daughter-in-law works, goes round for one day every week to look after her grandchildren. While she is there she always cooks something for their parents' supper that night and a few other dishes for the freezer, and the children love cooking with her. Grandparents who work themselves, or have other time-consuming commitments, cannot do this so often, but even on an occasional basis this kind of help is appreciated. Just make sure your daughter or daughter-in-law doesn't interpret your kindness as a slur on her housekeeping. Frances Partridge expressed the fears of many nervous grannies when she wrote: 'It's difficult to strike a happy balance between doing all one can, and longs to do, for those one loves, and backing gracefully off the stage. I see clearly the warning Ralph [her husband] would have been the first to give me: don't interfere in their lives.'

The first six months: the loneliness of the long-suffering parent

MUMS SAY:

I do find not having my parents living locally is difficult, not just from a practical point of view, but also because I think my daughter should see them more.

I was disappointed by the lack of immediate help, but they all work full time and live over 100 miles away… It just would have been handy to have a shoulder to lean on during the war zone that is having a newborn.

My parents live in the same small town, one and a half miles away and I walk there most weekdays, sometimes for an hour or so, sometimes for longer. My husband

works shifts and the help I get from Mum and Dad is invaluable.

It makes a huge difference to first-time mums if their own mother or mother-in-law lives within easy distance. Although grandparents can provide the valuable commodity of time off from the children, sometimes the greatest need for a young mum is company. Childcare can be a lonely business, especially after the second baby has arrived. One baby is, by comparison, easy. You sling it across your chest or hoist it into a backpack and off you go to meet your friends. Two children are a different story. The hassle of getting them both dressed for outdoors, then securely strapped into the car, or down the road and onto a bus, then out into a pram or buggy at the other end of the journey, can seem just too difficult. Even if your destination is only a walk away, getting there is no fun with a tired, cross toddler, with cold hands and a soggy mitten on a string trailing in the mud, wailing 'Carry! Carry!' while you are trying to push the baby's buggy across a busy road.

In this situation, company is the best thing a granny can provide. Outings to the supermarket or the park become easy with the help of another adult, and your company makes special expeditions, to an exhibition or to the swimming pool for example, not only possible, but pleasurable. Spending time with your daughter or daughter-in-law also gives you a chance to chat about your favourite topic: her children, your grandchildren.

MUMS SAY:
Since I had my children my relationship with my mum has changed completely – for the better. We have so much more in common now that I am going through the same peaks and troughs that she experienced.

We don't say much when we're together, but I just love seeing my mum with the children, and they seem to behave better when she's around.

Getting to know the baby

Many of us remember own grandmothers as somewhat remote, although loved and loving, and all agree that the greatest change from their generation to ours, apart from the fact that we have a longer expectation of life, and may therefore, with luck, see our grandchildren grow to adulthood, is that we are much more 'hands-on'.

You might think that, like riding a bicycle, you never quite forget how to look after a baby. You may imagine that, confronted with a baby, you will dredge up from your subconscious the necessary knowledge and skills.

But it is not so simple. In the thirty or so years since you bathed, fed, changed and put to sleep your own babies, ideas have moved on. Part of the reason for this book is to show you just how things have changed, and how you can best deal with the changes.

Babies can be alarming at first, especially for grandfathers.

A MUM SAYS:
My dad spends more time with his grandchildren than he did with his own children, since he has more free time now. He doesn't always get it spot on (after a poo in the potty last weekend, I saw him wiping her bottom with a Dettox wipe) but he tries his best and is only ever caring and patient.

In our generation it was unusual for men to be hands-on parents in the early stages, and many men feel awkward handling their first grandchild. But any nervousness of the baby will soon disappear. The more you hug him and cuddle him, the more the baby will respond, to grandfathers as well as grandmothers. The reassurance of being held firmly against a warm body is all the baby needs to bond with you. Don't be afraid to be demonstrative in the silliest ways. Making a fool of yourself doesn't matter. Put your face close to the baby's (their range of focus is very limited in the first few months), smile inanely and murmur foolish endearments. If you persevere you may be rewarded with a gummy smile. 'It's just wind', people in the know will say. But you don't have to believe them. The closer involvement of fathers and grandfathers with new babies is one of the greatest changes since our young days, and infinitely touching.

A MUM SAYS:
I love the way their grandparents spend as much time with them as they can, play with them, care for them in practical ways, and above all talk to them and show an interest in their lives, their hobbies and achievements.

A GRANNY SAYS:
The grandchildren have brought me utter joy and – just by being with us – made my life totally complete. I am besotted. Much more than I was with my children!

In the beginning your grandchild will spend a lot of time sleeping (God willing) and the times when he is alert and neither tired nor hungry will be all too fleeting, so make the most of them. As grandparents love to say, 'They grow up so fast', and you will get enormous pleasure from watching their growth and development at every stage. It is a delight and a privilege to see our grandchildren exploring the world, developing skills, learning to crawl, and speaking their first words. Tiny babies learn by imitation which means that, the more you smile and laugh at them, the more they will smile and laugh back, which will make you smile and laugh some more. A delicious circle.

When you are all together as a family, a ritual like 'pass the parcel' will probably take place, each player holding the baby for as long as he or she is allowed. But do resist the urge to hand the baby back to its parents as soon as it cries. 'Get hands-on,' a mum advises, 'change their nappies, cuddle them when they're crying as well as when they're happy.'

Calming a fretful baby is a skill we all had when our own children were infants. It will come back with a little practice and you will have a great sense of achievement if you can get the baby to sleep. Rocking and crooning are the best ways to comfort a distressed baby. The secret of success is endless repetition of regular, rhythmic movement. The theory is that you are reassuring the baby by imitating conditions in the womb. In there, there is very little space to move around, and babies seem to like being held close and tight. There is also a lot of motion, hence the success of rocking, jiggling up and down, and patting. Also, tests have shown, the noise in the womb is louder than the sound of a vacuum cleaner, which would account for the success some parents have in getting the baby off to sleep by hoovering the carpet.

You can croon any old rubbish that comes into your head, making it up as you go along. A single syllable repeated over and over works for me: 'shoo-shoo-shoo-shoo-shoo' I go, feeling a bit of an idiot if anyone is listening, or, if the baby can see my face, 'mum-mum-mum' (a gesture of female solidarity, in the hope that the baby will make this, rather than 'dad-dad-dad' his first utterance). If you prefer the tried and tested lullabies of your own and your children's childhood, but are a bit vague about the words, refresh your memory in the anthology on page 344.

If all else fails, crying babies sometimes settle if you take them out of doors for five minutes, or just to look out of the window. When the baby has fallen asleep in your arms or on your shoulder, unless you want go through the whole process again, make sure she is properly asleep before lowering her very gently into the crib or pram. You can be fairly sure when her head droops and her whole body feels heavy and relaxed.

Sometimes, when a baby cries persistently, the parents are as much in need of comforting as the baby. It is agonising for them to hear their child screaming and be powerless to help. But you, the granny, have seen it all before, and can at least reassure them. The best thing you can do is to take the baby out of earshot for a while, even if it's only into the next room. Remember that, whilst the baby's misery is distressing for you, too, at least, when you are worn out by the situation, you can go home and recover.

Alone together at last

The first time you are left alone to look after the baby, the parents will have briefed you about giving her the bottle, which nowadays may be full of breast-milk ('here's some I expressed earlier'); you will have their mobile phone numbers (how did we survive without them?) and the numbers of the doctor, the ambulance and the fire brigade.

Before you are left alone with the baby, make sure you watch one of the parents changing a nappy – better still, do a nappy change under the parent's supervision. The technique has changed since our day, but the change is for the better. You no longer run the risk of stabbing the baby with a safety pin, you no longer have to wash a dozen dirty nappies every day, and nappy bags make disposal a neat and tidy matter. Initially new grannies may be shocked at how seldom today's parents change their babies' nappies, but this is because modern nappies are designed in such a way that babies are not uncomfortable in a wet nappy, though they can still be miserable in a dirty one.

When putting the disposable nappy on the baby, all you need know is that the picture goes on the front, and the sealing tabs fasten in front; and that, once the nappy is secured, there should be space to slip your finger comfortably between the nappy and the baby's tummy. Don't leave the baby alone on the bed or changing mat – he might roll off. But you knew that already.

Nappy-free playtime is fun for the baby and for you. Before putting on the fresh nappy, allow time for stretching and kicking (draping a towel strategically, if the baby is a boy, to prevent a sudden drenching).

But what if the baby simply cries and will not be comforted? Yelling is his only way of letting you know something is wrong, so it is up to you to find out what it is.

Here is a check list:

• Is he hungry? How long ago was the last meal or bottle? Did the child finish it? If it is too soon to bring the next meal forward by twenty minutes or so, you could offer a snack or, with babies under 6 months, a bottle of water or juice, very much diluted. The parents probably have a rule about snacking between meals, but this may be an occasion when granny's rules apply.

• Thirsty? Offer water or juice.

• Wind? You remember what to do!

• Dirty nappy? Whether he needs it or not, going through the routine of a nappy change sometimes helps to settle a miserable baby.

• Too hot or too cold? A baby wrapped up in too many woollies will be itchy and uncomfortable. Feel the back of his neck to see if it is too hot or too cold, and take away or add a layer accordingly.

• Teething? If one cheek is redder than the other and the baby is dribbling, a new tooth may be on the way. The discomfort of teething is reduced if the baby has something to chew on. Rubbing the baby's gums gently with a clean finger can also help. If the baby is still fretful it does not harm to give the recommended dose of Calpol.

• Is he ill? If, ten minutes after taking off a layer or two of clothes, the baby still feels hot, he may have a fever. If you are worried, take his temperature. There is a new kind of thermometer you put in the child's ear. Babies can have temperatures as high as 104° F (40° C) without being in danger, but your instinct (you were a mother once, remember?) will tell you if your grandchild is seriously ill. If the fever does not respond to Calpol, or if you are in any doubt, call the doctor or NHS Direct.

• Tired? The most likely reason for prolonged crying is sheer fatigue. If it is bedtime you can cuddle and jiggle the baby until he falls asleep. But sometimes you need to keep a tired baby awake so he can eat before being put down for the night.

• Colic? Remember colic? Colic is a pain in the stomach prevalent in very small babies and sometimes lasting for hours at a time. Nobody knows what causes it, or how to soothe it. It usually clears up at about three months, but it is sometimes impossible to comfort a colicky baby. When we had our babies, gripe water was the remedy for colic. The thinking today is that, although administering it may have a psychological calming effect on the parents, it does nothing for the baby.

• Another possible cause of crying, not always considered, is simply boredom. Some babies settle better when entertained by the tune of a musical toy, others are fascinated by a mobile hanging over their cot, or a cloth book tied to the cot. It is good for everyone concerned if they become accustomed to entertaining themselves at an early age.

Putting the baby to bed

> *And she wrapped Him in swaddling clothes and laid him in a manger, because there was no room for them in the inn.*
>
> The Gospel according to St Luke, 2:7

Tiny babies are thought to derive comfort from being swaddled because having their limbs restrained is reassuringly like being in the womb, as described above. We did this when ours were tiny, although I never quite mastered the art of ending up with a tidy parcel – unlike Baby Jesus who, in some paintings of the Nativity, appears to be bandaged with strips of cloth like an Egyptian mummy. Your grandchild's parents will tell you their policy on swaddling with, if necessary, a demonstration.

Before leaving you alone with the baby, they will also tell you how wrong it is to put the baby to sleep in its pram or cot facing downwards. I did this with my babies, and you probably did with yours, because we knew no better. At the time it was considered a good idea; it was supposed to strengthen the child's neck and back. Now it is known to be dangerous and all babies must sleep on their backs, with their feet at the bottom of the cot or pram, rather than with their heads at the top. Follow the parents' routine with blankets or other covers. Mothers say that grannies are always worrying that they do not keep their babies wrapped up warm enough, but the modern idea is that, in the bad old days, babies were kept warmer than was good for them (yes, by us), and, although they should be in a warm room and out of draughts, they should not have blankets heaped on them.

Sod's Law will ensure that, when the parents' return from their evening out, the baby will be crying. She may have woken just two minutes before they walk in the door, or she may have been yelling inconsolably for half an hour. What you tell the parents is between you and your conscience.

The next stage: mum goes back to work

MUMS SAY:

Don't comment on the mum's decision to go back to work in a way that will increase the guilt she's already feeling. Things are very different from 20/30 years ago, and most households need that second income.

If my mum hadn't been around to look after him, I never would have gone back to work.

These days, after paid maternity leave, more than 50% of mothers of children under five go to work: one third work full time and two thirds work part time. This is very different from how things were for us, when working mothers were the exception, not the rule. You may not approve of your daughter or daughter-in-law going back to work so soon, but this, like many subjects you may feel like airing, comes under the heading 'none of your business'. If you are tempted to mention your misgivings, just remember that your grandchild's mum is likely to be sensitive on the subject.

And understandably. A recent international study, undertaken by the National Institute of Child Health and Human Development in the US, concluded that 'the more time children spend in childcare from birth to age four and a half, the more adults tended to rate them as less likely to get along with others, as more assertive, as disobedient and as aggressive'. In the UK, the University of London's Institute of Education reached a similar conclusion that: 'High levels of group care before the age of three (and particularly before the age of two) were associated with higher levels of anti-social behaviour at age three'.

Step forward, grannies and grandpas, there is clearly a role for you here. Indeed, many of you are already starring in it: the number of children benefiting from some form of grandparental care has gone from 33% to 82% in the last two generations.

The position of a regular childminder granny, of course, is different from that of a once-a-month or even a once-a-week granny. Instead of being the exciting giver of treats and outings, she is a mother substitute, with all the difficulties that implies. Naturally enough, some grannies find that, with the best will in the world, they are not able to take on the role. But for the granny who is both able and willing and has the time, the rewards are great. It is no coincidence that the word 'nanny' doubles up for a grandmother and for a child's nurse (let's leave female goats out of this). If you are your grandchild's part time nanny as well as granny, you will have the opportunity to form a uniquely close relationship, and have the pleasure, and sometimes the pain, of watching him grow and develop in close-up.

A granny friend who looks after her grandchildren every day offers this wise advice: 'Don't be afraid to be the short-tempered and crusty person you normally are. Children perceive hypocrisy quicker than anything else.' She also points out that children need to learn that grandparents get tired. This is particularly important if you are the routine carer and cannot, as more occasional grannies can, run yourself ragged and then retire and put your feet up, leaving the parents to cope while you recharge your batteries.

MUMS SAY:
I can't think of anyone I would trust more than my mother to look after my daughter. In many ways this would be the perfect outcome. I just have a nagging worry that it might be a bit much for her.

My mum tells me in exact detail everything they did together, what she ate, etc. etc. I don't think I would get this much information from say a nursery or child minder. Plus I know I can phone her several times a day if I want to.

My mum has just started to look after my son two

mornings a week. He loves his grandma so much and she just worships him. They do lots of things together – Tiny Gym, museums, park, stories – etc, etc. My mum is 64 and staggeringly fit. She loves looking after him and I feel so happy and relaxed knowing he is with her. No nanny could ever be the same.

My mother-in-law has my daughter three days a week when I work. She has good days and bad days (teething or just general strops!) and it knackers her out but she LOVES LOVES LOVES having her.

Getting to know them long-distance

If your grandchildren live so far away that it is difficult to get together regularly, don't despair. There are still ways you can communicate with them.

MUMS SAY:

Although my relationship with my parents is good, they rarely visit as they live over 200 miles away and are divorced and both busy with their new partners.

My parents are fantastic grandparents, despite never living closer than within $2^1/_2$ hours driving distance... my mum phones my boys every Saturday at a pre-arranged time, and they love telling her about their week.

Keeping in touch is a two-way business, involving telephone calls, letters, photographs and children's drawings. If distance is a problem, perhaps you can arrange to meet up halfway, two or three times a year. If you can only get together occasionally, Christmas is probably the worst time to choose, when everyone is on the move, other visits have to be fitted in and the children's minds are more on Father Christmas than granny and grandpa. It may be better to arrange a regular spring and early autumn weekend when, with a little luck, the weather will be good enough to spend time outdoors together.

Keeping in touch by telephone

Whereas it may be difficult to organise visits in either direction, the phone could not be easier. Most babies love the telephone. Even before they can talk they will make it their favourite toy if allowed to. If the phone rings and you answer it, and all you can hear is heavy breathing, don't hang up. It is not some stranger about to ask you what coloured knickers you are wearing – it is your grandchild, who doesn't realise that, unless she speaks, you don't know she is on the line.

When you phone the parents, make it seem as if you are really ringing the child – ask to speak to him first;

then, when you have finished your conversation, get him to pass the telephone to his mum or dad. Little ones love to hear your voice; it doesn't matter if the conversation is one-sided or if you are talking rubbish, just gabble away telling them what you have been doing, how your dog and cat are, what is growing in the garden, anything you can think of. When they are a little older, they will chat away to you about what is happening at home and at school. Encourage your grandchildren to get in the habit of ringing you up to tell you their news: 'Guess what, granny, I drawed a picture of you,' or 'I got a star at school today,' or 'I'm going to Ellen's birthday party tomorrow.'

Keeping in touch by post:

A MUM SAYS
My mum sends them little things in the post all the time, and they adore getting envelopes addressed to themselves. Now they can read and write they enjoy responding.

A GRANDCHILD WRITES:
Dear granny, when you read this a kiss will jump on your face.

Children love getting letters or cards. If there is more than one child, it is important to be even-handed. You can send postcards any time, not just when on holiday. If you have a special interest you'd like your grandchildren to share, you can start fostering it by sending them cards of paintings, animals, flowers, or whatever your speciality is. When they start to read, write very legibly in simple words, but in lower case letters, not capitals. Nowadays they learn their alphabet that way.

Equally, this generation is probably skilled on the computer before they can write. If you or your co-grand-parents haven't mastered receiving and sending e-mails and text messages yet, shame on you.

GRANDCHILDREN SAY:
My brother and I got left with our grandparents a lot, and those weeks I spent with them were some of the most special of my whole childhood. Sometimes kids need a holiday from their parents too!

I wish I could stay at Nana and Gramp's for ever and ever.

Their place or yours?

Sooner or later the question may arise whether it is better, when you are looking after your grandchildren, for you to go to their house or for them to come to yours.

Most grandparents and parents agree that small babies

are best cared for in their own familiar environment, whereas older babies and toddlers enjoy being in the different surroundings that you can offer along with different toys to play with.

Some grandparents feel quite strongly that they prefer their own base: 'I know where to lay my hands on everything', 'It's easier for me to cook', 'I don't like London', 'It's best if they come to me because relationships are strained'.

A few grannies admit to wanting to stay in their own houses simply for reasons of space and comfort. Their explanations are mostly expressed in mild language: 'The comfort rate is a bit higher at our house!!' or 'Their place is a bit chaotic', but two grannies used the phrase 'absolute tip' to describe their daughters' homes. Interestingly, only one mum felt that way about her own mother's house: 'I prefer it when she comes to me because my place is so much cleaner and better ordered.'

Either way, happily, it seems the parents of the children often agree that granny's place is best. One area of possible contention is whether the grandchild comes with an accompanying au pair or nanny. Families may think they are doing the grandparents a kindness if the helper comes too, but this arrangement is not always welcomed by grandparents:

A GRANNY SAYS:
Friends of mine will only have their grandchildren to stay (without parents) if they come with a 'keeper'. On the contrary, I won't have a keeper – they are far more trouble! Also I feel one gets much closer to the children without any other distractions. I have a lovely relationship with our grandchildren and often have them here for quite a long time, giving the parents a break. We have great fun and I love it.

As this granny implies, 'keepers' have to be cooked for and talked to, and shown the way around your kitchen. They may well be more trouble than they are worth, so if this kind of arrangement is on offer, you may want to think carefully before you accept it.

Think carefully, in fact, before agreeing to take sole charge of the children at all. I cannot say often enough that you should never feel obliged to do so if it doesn't suit your plans. As one mum explained, 'Crucially, my mother-in-law sometimes refuses, so that I know it is all right when she agrees.' If you feel that it's all right to say 'no' occasionally, the parents can be confident, when they ask you on other occasions, that they are not imposing on you.

'I love having them to stay without their parents,' one

granny says. 'I've always found the children easier to manage without the parents,' says another. Grandparents are almost unanimous in agreeing with this. The complex emotional agenda and power struggle between parent and child just doesn't exist between grandparents and grandchildren.

As a result it is relatively easy for grandparents to persuade children to behave acceptably and to abide by whatever gentle rules are imposed. There is little, if any, of the sulking, whinging and answering back that inevitably happens when they are at home.

Indeed, as children grow older, they are usually glad of an occasional respite from family life. In some families the children are under constant pressure from their parents and schools to perform and achieve. A holiday from such stress is one of the greatest benefits the Good Granny can offer her grandchildren. So don't try and do too much when your grandchildren come to stay. The best thing you can do for them may be simply to provide a rest from trying to live up to expectations – don't be too demanding, and if you do have high expectations yourself, don't reveal them. (On a similar note, when you are with your grandchild, you will often find yourself thinking, 'Oh, I do love you so much'. *Do* allow yourself to say it out loud. Diffidence about showing emotion is a well-known characteristic of the English and many of us find it difficult to outwardly express love and affection. I don't remember my own parents telling me they loved me, although I know they did, and I don't think I spoke to my children of my love for them, but it seems easy and natural to tell your grandchildren how much you love them, and it is unlikely to embarrass them.)

When it comes to having your grandchildren to stay, try and make a point of ringing the changes a bit. Having one child alone, for example, can do wonders both for your relationship and theirs with their own family; though it goes without saying that grandparents must be even-handed and, if you have one child to stay solo, you must have the others in turn. (see 'Favouritism' on page 301).

Also, if you have the space and can cope with it, you can use longer visits to get them together with their cousins. Cousinship can be a strong bond forged in childhood to last a lifetime, and it is an important function of grandparents to make sure cousins have the chance to get to know each other well. It is a delight to see your grandchildren from different families forming friendships, and they often find it easier on your neutral ground than in the home of either cousin.

A GRANNY SAYS:
For a while one of my grandsons didn't get on at all well with his cousin, but I ignored it and continued to have them both to stay with me together. Now they have matured a bit they have become inseparable!

First nights

The first time you look after your grandchildren on your own for more than an occasional night at their house or yours, you will probably be apprehensive. A grandfather described his feelings as the last couple of hours ticked away before his daughter departed for a week's holiday as, 'The same as I feel before a dentist's appointment.' The parents will also have agonised over the idea of the visit before they ask you to have your grandchildren to stay. It is not that they don't trust you, more that they cannot believe their children can be entirely happy in their absence.

One mum told me of the deep anxiety she felt when she and her husband decided to celebrate their wedding anniversary with a long weekend in Spain, leaving the children with her mum and dad. Rosie (2) adores them, but five days was a long time for her to be away from her mother. She need not have worried. She took the good advice of friends, and made it crystal clear to Rosie that mummy and daddy were coming back. She and her husband also wrapped up five small presents each for Rosie and her little brother Ben, so they could open one every day in their absence. .

When our children were little and my husband went away on business, he always brought back presents; when he came home, he could hardly get the front door open before they rushed headlong at him, grasping his legs and crying: 'Wot have you bwought us, dad?'

Saying goodbye

When your grandchild's parents go away leaving him with you, the moment of parting can be tricky however much he loves you. Some children take it in their stride. They can scarcely be bothered to look up from the game they are playing. But others find it very upsetting to say goodbye. If your grandchild is like this, at the words 'Be a good boy for granny' and 'We'll be back very soon' you can expect his face to crumple. If you can use your skill in distraction tactics to good effect all may be well. But it does not work every time, and you may be faced with a screaming child, in deep distress, clinging desperately to his mother's legs.

I am describing a scenario I have been through myself,

when I witnessed what I can only describe as projectile weeping: tears shot almost horizontally from my grandson's eyes. Crying is catching, and his mother's lip began to wobble, and I found myself losing control of my voice as well as my tear ducts.

In this situation you must act quickly to detach your grandchild from his mother, even if it means using force. Shoo the parents out of the house, with a promise to call them on their mobile in 20 minutes and shut the door behind them. This is your grandchild's cue for even louder wailing. It is your cue to offer him chocolate or whatever his treat of treats is, and hold him in a close hug until the sobbing subsides, as it eventually will, leaving an occasional hiccup in its wake. Blowing his nose is advisable, and washing the face with a cool flannel has a soothing effect after serious crying. On the occasion I describe, after the chocolate and the face-wash my grandson settled down very cheerfully to drawing and cutting out, occasionally remembering to let me know, in a reproachful voice, 'I'm still sad, Granny Jane.'

The misery your grandchild feels at the moment of separation from his parents is unlikely to recur if you and he have a close and loving relationship, but it pays to be on the lookout for a wobbly lip or drooping shoulders, especially towards the end of the day when he is tired.

If you are ready with a diversion you can avoid the bad moment. If homesickness does turn out to be a problem, it helps to make a big calendar to tick off the days. This is something you can do together, cutting out, sticking and colouring pictures for each day.

Phoning home: 'I miss you mummy'

As soon as they are able to say more than a few words, modern children become accustomed to speaking to their parents on the telephone, and they will certainly want to do so when the parents are away. This is generally thought not to be a good idea, on the grounds that most children will be perfectly happy without their parents until they hear their voices. But it is hard to deny a determined child the pleasure of talking to his mother and father when he knows that it is perfectly possible to do so.

Things have changed a great deal in this respect. When I was a child, telephones were only for grown-ups. A transcontinental call was only ever used to break bad news. But today parents and grandparents think nothing of calling from the Antipodes to chat to a toddler about what he had for lunch, and whether it has rained today.

So, when your grandchildren stay with you, a daily telephone call is almost inevitable, however ill-advised. You will probably find that the only moment they show any signs at all of missing their parents is while they are talking to them, or when they have just finished the telephone call. If weeping and wailing start while mum or dad is still listening at the other end of the line, the best thing you can do is limit the damage by snatching the receiver out of the child's hand; say 'she's absolutely fine really, I'll call you after she's in bed,' and ring off before they can reply.

This is another moment for distraction tactics. Take a balloon out of your pocket and blow it up, or trot round to the corner shop for a tube of Smarties. Try to have a pre-arranged routine for phone calls. If international time zones permit, the morning is the best time, when there is a busy day of having fun in front of you, rather than at bedtime when your grandchild will be tired and vulnerable.

A MUM SAYS:
We've left our three-year-old with both sets of grand-

parents several times for up to three days. He's always been fine, never missed us in the slightest – too busy having fun and getting spoiled rotten. We always play up the 'You're going for a special trip to Grandma's,' rather than, 'Mummy and daddy are going away'.

A GRANNY SAYS:
We had the grandchildren for a week and they were absolutely fine. There was one wobbly moment at bedtime on the third day, but when the time came to leave, Robert cried because he wanted to stay longer.

When the parents get home, they may find their child intractable, difficult and bad-tempered. This is *not* the grandparents' fault. The child is paying her parents back for leaving her, and may sulk for a bit just as your cat does if you have been away for a few days.

At your place: a safe house.

MUMS SAY:
The only thing I nag my mother about is safety – shutting the garden gate, not leaving the bathwater in, not opening the windows fully, etc. I feel the house is a huge potential hazard to those not familiar with the possible dangers for small children.

She never clears dangerous things away so I have to watch the children all the time.

Some parents are convinced that grandparents have no idea about safety in the home, and it may be true that many of us have forgotten what we knew perfectly well thirty or forty years ago. Even then, not all parents could be trusted. Here are a couple of cautionary tales.

On one occasion, a little girl of two was left in a sitting room where there was a low cupboard full of wine glasses. The drinks tray sat on top of it. When her mother came back into the room, little Sophy was sitting on the floor in front of the open cupboard in a nest of smashed and splintered glass. There was no blood to be seen; miraculously she appeared not to have cut herself. But what if she had put glass in her mouth? What if she had swallowed it?

Her mum scooped her up, flew to the car and dashed to the local hospital's Casualty Department. The young doctor in charge suggested a diet of bread and bananas to mop up any glass splinters inside her and ease them out. As it turned out, nothing happened, except that Sophy refused to eat bananas for several months.

That happened 39 years ago. Sophy's parents still have the same cupboard and it is still full of wine glasses. Now it is their grandchildren who are at risk, but they have learned to tie the two cupboard door handles together with a ribbon or string, so they cannot be opened by little fingers. Most cupboards in the house get this treat ment because none of the floor level cupboards seem to have locks, or else the keys are missing. One cupboard has a handle missing as well as the key. This one gets sealed with strips of masking tape, which sticks securely enough to deter little fingers but is easily removed when access is needed.

The second 'accident', about six months later, was potentially even more dangerous. Sophy's younger broth-er was alone in his mum's bedroom for just long enough for her to go to the loo (such a luxury, to go alone). She returned to find, spilt on the floor, a bottle of Thawpit, a highly poisonous solvent stain remover. She scolded him for spilling it and put him down for his nap. An hour later, when she went to wake him, his face was white and his lips were blue. This time she drove to the hospital with her fist on the car hooter all the way. There was a stomach pump and several dreadfully anxious hours. The baby survived and the doctor severely reprimanded the mother.

I describe these incidents simply to remind you how horribly easy it is to be careless. Our children are very conscientious about locking away kitchen and bathroom poisons, and we must make sure we are too: 'More than one-third of medicine poisonings are due to children taking their grandparents' prescription drugs. Check to be sure the grandparents' medicines are locked away or completely out of reach before the children arrive for a visit.' (*Dr Spock's Baby and Child Care*. Revised edition 1998)

> *You see, how could young Goldie know,*
> *For nobody had told her so,*
> *That Grandmama, her old relation,*
> *Suffered from frightful constipation.*
> *This meant that every night she'd give*
> *Herself a powerful laxative,*
> *And all the medicines that she'd bought*
> *Were naturally of this sort.*
>
> Roald Dahl

Small children are fascinated by keys, and, given half a chance, will lock themselves into the loo or the bathroom. When one two-year-old I know accomplished this, the fire brigade had to be called to extricate him, and a new door fitted at exorbitant cost. The longterm solution to the problem is to install bolts or fastening hooks high up on the door, out of childish reach. In the short term, all you can do is hide keys, unscrew and remove bolts, and tell grown-ups to sing loudly while they are in occupation.

Here is a quick checklist of the boring safety stuff:

• Turn the cooker, dishwasher, washing machine and tumble dryer off at the main switches except when you are using them (this is one I always forget). When cooking, use the back burners rather than front, and turn handles of pots inwards, out of reach. Make sure knives are not accessible. Check window catches are out of reach and don't open the bottom half of a sash window.

• Move all breakable ornaments, potted plants and flower vases out of reach. 'Out of reach' means not just out of the reach of a child standing on the floor, but out of reach when standing on a sofa or chair.

• You can't turn your whole house into a padded cell, but if your grandchildren have not yet learned how to negotiate stairs safely, do block them off at top and bottom. If it is not practical to install gates, at least put a mattress at the bottom for a soft landing. If the parents have not already done so, it is worth spending time teaching your grandchildren to crawl downstairs backwards.

- If you have an open fireplace, use a sturdy and secure fireguard. Hide firelighters, matches and lighters.

> *Billy in one of his nice new sashes*
> *Fell in the fire and was burnt to ashes.*
> *Now, although the nights grow chilly,*
> *I haven't the heart to poke poor Billy.*
> Harry Graham, *Ruthless Rhymes for Heartless Homes*

If there is dirt at floor level, a crawling baby will certainly find it, and probably eat it, so the house should be kept reasonably clean, however easy-going you normally are about such things. The reassuring words 'A little dirt never did anyone any harm' were often heard a few decades ago, but the phrase cuts no ice with the new generation of parents. On the other hand, obsessive cleanliness is not necessarily a good thing either. According to a recent study, 'Air freshener and aerosols with polish, deodorant, hairspray can cause diarrhoea in babies and earache in young children. Possibly also headaches and depression in adults: 40% of British households use these products.' (Bristol University, *Children of the 90s* study.) In some households there is no risk of obsessive cleanliness. One mum told me how, when she opened the front door one morning to her mother-in-law, her toddler trotted down the passage, beaming and brandishing the loo brush. Her mother-in-law looked horrified. 'Don't worry,' said the mum, 'It's never been used.'

A MUM SAYS:
Jessica has an extremely close relationship with her grandparents. She has her own cot, sleeping bag and highchair at their place. She is so comfortable and happy there that there is no problem with leaving her overnight.

If you can build up a stock of equipment, it will save your family a lot of trouble packing the car each time they visit you. How many big items you want to borrow or buy depends on how much space you have to store them, and how frequent the visits are. Friends and relations may be glad to pass on a cot, a high chair, a pram or a car seat, all of which will be useful at one time or another. If you can get hold of a pushchair, you can spend the long winter evenings practising folding and unfolding it, thus avoiding humiliation when you come to use it. You shouldn't have to buy anything new. 'Ebay', small-ads in the local paper, and car-boot sales are good sources.

Among worthwhile smaller items, you might consider getting a baby monitor. New since our day, these marvellous gadgets can none the less give you the shock of your life if you are not used to them: ours picks up conversations our neighbours' children are having in their bedroom across the road, rather than our grandchildren upstairs.

Basically, the more stuff you can supply, the easier it will be for your family to visit you. An electric bottle-warmer can be useful, as well as smaller items such as babies' bottles and drinking cups, plastic bowls and spoons for toddlers. A non-slip mat for the bath is good, and, for toddlers, a potty and/or a child's loo seat that fits on top of the adult one.

Grandparents tend to get more excited about toilet training than parents. When our grandchildren reached this stage I rushed out and bought a potty for every room but they remain unchristened. The grandchildren used the 'big loo' from the (rather late) start.

Do as much shopping as you can before grandchildren arrive for a visit. Buy in enough nappies, wipes, etc, to last the course. Check with the parents what type of formula or milk, your grandchildren's favourite breakfast cereal, what juice, white bread or brown, what kinds of fruit and vegetables they will eat. You will also get through an amazing amount of kitchen paper (how did we ever manage before it was invented?), cleaning sticky hands and wiping noses. And for first aid: plasters (you can get decorative ones, sometimes useful to distract a child who is not hurt at all); Savlon cream or other disinfectant; wasp-eze; Calpol.

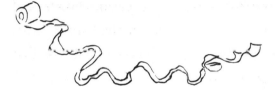

Granny's toys

> Oscar's mum: '*Which of your toys shall we pack to take to Granny and Grandpa's house?*'
> Oscar (scornfully): '*Granny has her own toys.*'

Strictly speaking, you don't really need toys. You already have saucepans, wooden spoons, plastic containers with lids, plastic bottles, mixing bowls in assorted sizes and yoghurt pots. You also have newspapers, magazines and, if you saved them, picture postcards and Christmas and birthday greetings cards.

Nevertheless, children enjoy finding different toys at

granny and grandpa's house, and look forward to being reunited with them, so it is worth keeping a small selection for appropriate ages. There is no need to spend a fortune; you can beg hand-me-downs from friends or search in charity shops and car-boot sales. Granny's toys and granny's books are kept at granny's house, and not to be taken home. The following have been much used by our grandchildren over a wide age span, giving us much appreciated spells of peace and quiet: wooden building bricks and a plastic lorry to transport them; a good quality stacking plastic toy and a posting toy; a medium-sized soft ball which makes electronic noises when you catch it, kick it or drop it; a cheap plastic cooking set with toy cooker and pots, plates and cutlery.

If you can't bear garish plastic toys which play nursery rhymes or messages from outer space when you push the buttons, this is your chance to assert your superior taste by buying classic wooden toys like the rowing boat with nine round men (eight plus the cox) to slot into their places. It is on wheels so that a toddler can pull it along. A toy telephone can be popular for a while, but most children much prefer the real thing, whether it is a land-line or your mobile. Care is needed, as toddlers have been known, by trial and error, to get through to the Emergency Services who, quite naturally, are not amused. A torch is another popular non-toy plaything. A block of wood, a hammer (adult size) and some large nails were the favourite playthings of one of our grandsons at the age of three. Another, at about the same age, became bored with washing his toy tractor, much preferring to wash my car, or at least the parts he could reach.

A bunch of keys is an irresistible toy and can be useful to distract a child at a stressful moment, for example when it is time to say goodbye to mummy. But if a toddler hides your keys or drops them you may never see them again, so make sure you retrieve them and put them in a safe place, out of reach. A granny tells how she gave her grandson her daughter's car and house keys to play with at a moment of stress, then took them from the child and hid them in a safe place. She then completely forgot about them (as grannies do). When the time came to take the children home, the house was turned upside down searching for her keys but they were nowhere to be found. They all had to go home by train. Eighteen months later, dusting the top of a high bookshelf, granny discovered the keys. The moral of the story is, if you have a 'safe place', remember it. And if you think you can't remember it, write it down.

Other favourite playthings that disappear from time to time are the TV zapper and the little plastic Sky TV card.

If the card goes missing, look in the video slot. You won't be able to get your big hand in to retrieve it, so you will have to persuade the child who put it in, to get it out himself.

After your keys and the TV zapper, the most popular toy will be your glasses, if you wear them. Little babies are fascinated by them and as soon as they have the necessary skill, will snatch them off your nose. Quite cute the first time, but infuriating (and expensive in terms of replacements) when repeated again and again and again. A firm 'No' said with a frown is the correct response the very first time and, if necessary, repeatedly.

What to expect: a low boredom threshold (theirs)

Children can't concentrate for long (unless you want them to come and eat, or put their coats on to go out, in which case they can become totally engrossed in their train set or their favourite video for long enough for you to become quite cross). They also find it confusing to be offered too much choice.

When confronted with a floor littered with toys, they sometimes home in on a favourite, but they are more likely to keep choosing and rejecting different playthings until they become bored with the whole lot. The answer is to offer just a few to choose from, get down on the floor and join in the game. The short attention span is inevitable. Nobody in their right mind, of any age, wants to stack up the stacking cups more than three or four times running, and the same goes for doing and undoing a jigsaw with just eight large pieces. When interest in the toys begins to flag, a story read aloud, or a picture book to which you can make up the words, goes down well. There is no need to restrict reading to bedtime, and it gives you the chance of a delicious cuddle on the sofa.

You can't always predict what will get a child's imagination started, but in my experience they tend to remain absorbed longer with fantasy games. I have seen a two-year-old form a passionate attachment to a small basket, not intended as a toy at all. It sparked off a game of shopping which lasted on and off all day. Only the basket was 'real'. The nearest adult played the parts of butcher, baker and candlestick-maker. The meat, the bread and buns, the candlesticks and the fruit and veg. at the greengrocer's were all imaginary, as was the money which changed hands.

What to expect: a low boredom threshold (yours)
On the whole, the smaller the child the more limited the attention span, but there are a few games of which they never seem to tire. So be prepared to play peek-a-boo,

build a castle for your grandchild to knock down, or throw a ball for him to catch, or fail to catch, again and again and again. Have a trump card up your sleeve ready to play when you are pushed across the boredom threshold. Getting out the vacuum cleaner, loading or unloading the washing machine, or feeding the cat are effective diversionary ploys. Or you can simply offer a snack if it is not too near lunch-time.

It's unlikely to be anywhere near lunchtime. Time never flies when you are childminding. When you begin to feel bored or exhausted or both, and look at your watch to see if it's time for your grandchild's nap, you will be amazed to find that only an hour has passed since breakfast and you have three more hours to fill until lunch. Your feelings of boredom and weariness are probably also tinged with guilt. You think you are a good granny, so why aren't you getting more enjoyment out of being one?

The answer is that you have not yet allowed yourself to regress fully to childhood. You are still treating time in a grown-up way, with part of your brain preoccupied with chores that need to be done, telephone calls that need to be made, bills that need to be paid. The cure is to suspend your perception of time, and think yourself back to a time when birthdays and Christmas took aeons to come round, and it seemed as if tomorrow would never come. It is a luxury to allow time to stand still for a day, and to slow down accordingly. It is wonderful for children, who lead rather hectic lives with their parents, to be with granny who is never in a hurry, and it is good for you too. You probably lead an equally hectic life, and will benefit from putting it on hold. So empty your mind of mundane concerns, enter your grandchild's world and enjoy it.

Exhaustion (yours and theirs)

No matter how relaxed you are, you will find, when the children take a nap, you need one too. If a nap is no longer part of the routine, insist on a 'Quiet Time'. It can be spent with your feet up, reading to each other. Reading comes near the top of the list of things grannies enjoy doing with their grandchildren. If you are too tired to read, the 'Quiet Time' is as good an excuse as any for watching television or a video – though this is a fraught issue for many of today's parents (See WHAT SHALL WE DO AT HOME? The last resort, page 208)

Either way, don't try to be supergran all the time. Life

with an energetic toddler is wearing. Do allow yourself some self-indulgent recovery time, when you can go to bed early after a leisurely bath, and don't organise a busy schedule the following day.

Bearing gifts

Giving presents is one of the pleasures of being a grandparent. At Christmas and on birthdays, we love to see their faces light up when they tear the wrapping paper off their parcels, confirming that we have chosen well. 'Wow' and 'just what I wanted' are music to our ears.

But, much as you want to create a big splash, try and check that you have got it right. You want the pet, the ice skates, the drum kit, the bicycle, the computer, the tennis racquet, the kung-fu tuition to be a wonderful birthday surprise to your grandchild, and so it can be. But don't let it be a surprise to the parents.

If you are better off than your children, you may want to offer to give the 'main' present, but do make the offer tactfully and if it is not well received, withdraw gracefully.

Parents greatly appreciate being consulted

about what to give for Christmas and birthdays. Most young families live in houses already bursting at the seams as far as storage space goes, and last Christmas when I asked my daughter the reply was 'Just nothing too big, please, mum.'

A GRANNY SAYS:
I don't think I am mean but I take the view that my grandchildren have lots of toys and clothes already, and really don't need more from me. I usually arrive empty handed and when I do bring a small present, it might be something like a fossil picked up when weeding the garden.

MUMS SAY:
My grandmother always bought the big birthday or Christmas present. It was a source of huge excitement.

At Christmas both sets of grandparents compete to be the biggest spenders, and our presents and Santa's pale into insignificance.

Girls and Boys: guns and dolls

What are little girls made of?
Sugar and spice, and all thing nice,
That's what little girls are made of.
What are little boys made of?

Slugs and snails and puppy dogs' tails,
That's what little boys are made of.

'Politically correct' is a phrase which had little or no meaning when we were bringing up our children. How things have changed. Now, one mum is incensed that her mother-in-law gave her daughter a doll's pram for her birthday; another praises hers for giving a toy hoover to her son.

My observation tells me that most little girls are quite straightforwardly less keen on train sets than little boys, nor do they pick up a stick, brandish it and yell to their male cousin, 'Let's kill Granny Jane!' I don't think many parents would offer odds on which toy a small boy would choose if put in a room with a toy garage and a Barbie doll complete with accessories. But I also believe it is tactful to keep quiet about all this because if I were to voice my opinion the parents of my grandchildren would think I was stuck in the dark ages.

Buying clothes

To give clothes on your own initiative to older children, you need to be very confident that your taste is the same as that of the parents and of the child, and that you are filling a gap in their wardrobe rather than giving

If you are uncertain what to give, and have not had sight of the wish-list posted up the chimney to Father Christmas, here is a list of best and worst presents suggested by parents and grandparents:

Best presents

Stacking cups
A walker to push, full of wooden bricks
Toy hoover
Toy baby's buggy
Rocking horse
Rocking chair
Books
Brio train set
Bow and arrow
Lego
Duplo
Farmyard
Snakes and Ladders
Lion King DVD
A watch on a chain
Indian dressing-up clothes
Leap-pad electronic reader
Electric toothbrush
Subscription to a good comic
Trampoline
Home-knitted blanket

Worst presents

Most cuddly toys
Box of beads given to a 2-year-old
Huge Easter eggs
A really scary rag doll
Playhouse (unless there is plenty of space)
Huge plastic garage
Huge anything
A doll's pram just because she is a girl
Anything that makes repetitive loud noises, or requires frequent battery changes
Clothes

redundant garments. If you want your present to be a surprise but are in doubt about the style, the answer is to buy it from a shop where it can be returned without fuss.

However, mums vary in their attitudes. One is very firm, and advises, 'Don't buy clothes unless you can do it on a shopping trip with the mum; your tastes and hers will never coincide so the clothes probably won't get used.' But another remembers the fun of conspiring with her grandmother to thwart her mother: 'When pedal-pushers were in, my Mum wouldn't let me have them so Nana got them! And a ra-ra skirt! I can see how my mother might have been really cheesed off but it didn't do me any lasting damage and I LOVED IT!!' If you are a Glam Gran or Rock'n'Roll Gran, this is probably the line you prefer to take. Another mum describing her mother-in-law's generosity says, admiringly rather than disapprovingly, 'The clothes, my god, I can't get the wardrobe shut.'

Giving money

When we were children we became used to hoping for, even expecting, a tip from our grandfathers each time we saw them. It might be a shiny florin, a ten-shilling note, or, on a birthday, a fantastically generous large, white fiver.

You still can't go wrong with cash for older children who are saving up to buy themselves something they have set their heart on, but if you are giving large sums to teenagers, make sure the parents know – I heard of one granny who was inadvertently financing her grandson's drug habit.

Grandparents who want to look after their grandchildren by contributing to their longterm financial security, should also make their arrangements known to the parents, and preferably consult them before embarking on any savings scheme. Their generosity may affect decisions the parents have to make about such matters as school fees.

I cannot do more than briefly touch on the subject, but if you have not already done so, you might like to leave your grandchildren something in your Will. 'I was really pleased to be remembered in their Wills,' a granddaughter writes, 'not for the financial aspect but because I feel it confirmed what I had always thought – that we were very important to them in their lives.'

It isn't always fun

Let's be honest and admit that sometimes our grandchildren disappoint us. We look forward to seeing them so much, imagining a perfect hour, day or week with them.

But it is not always like that. The children may no longer want to do the things you looked forward to. They grow out of toys and games they once loved. For a lot of the time we are tired and cross, and the children may be too. If we have got them for a week, at the end of the first day we wonder how we are going to get through six more days. They say 'I want' instead of 'Please' and 'Thank you'; they whinge for sweets, biscuits and videos; they ignore you when you ask them to do something; a nose or a bottom always needs wiping; on some days, whatever you suggest doing the answer is, 'Don't want to.' In short, they sometimes seem rude, boring, spoilt, unattractive or badly brought up. Or all of these things. And we are thoroughly disenchanted.

We feel like this because we start out with unrealistic expectations. We may have fallen into the trap of thinking that we can do better than their parents in some departments of behaviour management. We have probably forgotten that we ourselves were found wanting in various aspects of child-rearing a generation ago. The way out of these doldrums is to laugh at yourself and to give your grandchildren each a big hug and a kiss. And perhaps an unsolicited chocolate biscuit. The pleasure of giving a treat is so much greater if it is given when least expected, rather than as a response to nagging.

Nor should you let yourselves be unduly put out if, when it comes to saying goodbye to them, they seem singularly graceless and unappreciative.

I am ashamed to say that it gives me a little thrill of pleasure when, as has happened very occasionally, my grandchildren cry when it is time to go home from our house. I can't help feeling pleased that the visit has been such a success for them.

But just as often, having established and demonstrated a wonderfully loving relationship during their visit, the grandchildren, as soon as their parents appear to take them home, transfer their affections instantly, and hardly give you another thought. Don't let this worry you. It is absolutely right and natural that their parents come first, and it doesn't mean they don't love you dearly.

CHAPTER 5 – GETTING ABOUT

James James said to his mother,
'Mother' he said, said he,
'You must never go down to the end of the town
'If you don't go down with me.'

A.A. Milne

On foot

As I wrote earlier, the best thing you can do for parents is to give them a rest from their children. Even if you only spend an hour walking to the shops and back, or round the local park, it is a golden hour for the parents, and can be a golden hour for you too: a chance to bond, one to one, with your grandchild.

If your grandchild is still an infant, you can have a happy time together provided she is not hungry, so make sure she has a full tank before you start. You might think that, if the baby is being breastfed, and nowadays this may continue well beyond the first six months, the time she can spend away from her mother will be restricted to the time between feeds. It is not necessarily so. Most breast-feeding mums keep a supply of their milk in the fridge or freezer, and decant it into a bottle for just such an occasion: another example of how things have changed. A mother who came to stay with us left a bottle of her own milk in our fridge when she went home. It didn't seem right to pour it down the sink, and posting it back to her in a parcel seemed out of the question, so I put it in the freezer, where it still awaits her next visit.

You can take the baby in her pram, or even sling her across your chest. In communities where childcare is non-existent and parents have to return to work as soon as possible after their babies are born, the child is more often carried on the mother's back, leaving greater freedom for tilling the fields. But back or front, or slung on the hip, the principle is the same.

The nearest you will get to tilling fields is probably a visit to the local pick-your-own fruit farm, but if your grandchild's parents have a baby sling, do use it. Carrying a baby in this way is like a prolonged cuddle with hands free. My daughter-in-law has a wonderfully simple, very basic affair, just a wide, jersey tube which, when slung across one shoulder, forms a kind of hammock across the mother's (or grandmother's) front. Other slings are more like carrying harnesses and can be complicated to put on. But, whichever kind of sling you use, they are great for tiny babies, and the rhythmic movement as you walk will probably send them to sleep. With a more structured sling, the baby is held upright, and, if she is facing your chest, should soon fall asleep. Slightly older babies can be carried facing outwards, and, when wide awake and alert, will enjoy seeing the world go by. I feel very modern and trendy carrying my grandchildren in this way, and exchanging conspiratorial smirks with parents or other grannies pushing prams or pushchairs.

You can also get baby rucksacks to carry on your back, for babies over six months, when they can hold their heads up. They are useful for carrying older babies when the terrain is too rough for a pushchair, even of the sporty cross-country type, but beware – they can become rather heavy when filled with a well-nourished 11-month-old!

When our grandchildren were babies, a friend lent us an old-fashioned pram to keep at our house for their visits. It was of the type that used to be known as a 'baby carriage', high off the ground with springs and large wheels, and came with a fringed, linen sunshade and a net to protect the baby from cats. It had already served two generations of babies, and I used it the way my mother used hers, wheeling it into the garden and parking it under a tree, so the baby could enjoy the dappled shifting of the leaves against the sky. Today's mothers are shocked at the idea of leaving a baby alone in the garden, so perhaps you should ask their permission, explaining that the pram can be seen from the kitchen window, and promising to go out and look at the baby every ten minutes.

If you are taking a toddler further than the letterbox or the corner shop, taking the buggy with you is strongly recommended, even if your grandchild initially insists on walking. You don't want to have to carry her home, and the buggy provides useful carrying space for all the paraphernalia that you need. Always go armed with a drink, in one of those lidded mugs which didn't exist in our day, and a snack. If your grandchild has a comfort blanket or toy, woe betide you if you forget to bring it along. Before leaving home always make sure babies have clean nappies and make toddlers go to the loo. A useful gadget, not available to us first time around, when a buggy was known as a pushchair, is the buggy board – a platform fixed behind the buggy on which a tired older child can stand while a younger sibling rides in the buggy.

Going equipped

In your pocket:

• Tissues, particularly during the snot season, which is term time all the year round and holidays as well except in summer.

• A few sweets if allowed, or raisins, as emergency comforters or rewards.

• Small toys or curiosities to bring out for distraction tactics or crisis-management if you sense a tantrum coming on: e.g. snail's shell, balloon, plastic dinosaur or other cereal-packet toy.

In a backpack or Miss-Prism-sized handbag:

• Most mothers keep a backpack ready, and hand it to the grandparent with the baby. It contains a spare nappy, wipes and clean trousers. Add a bottle or spill-proof mug of milk, formula, juice or water, depending on the baby's age and routine, breadsticks, rice cakes or other snacks.

• Optional extras: band-aids and in winter, scarves and gloves; plastic bags for *objets trouvés*. If you are taking the dog, plastic bags anyway. If you plan to stop at a café, scrap paper, crayons and books.

It is second nature to grandparents, and gives them pleasure to do things for their grandchildren, like buttoning them into their coats and easing little feet into boots. But for parents, getting children ready to go out is a tiresome chore, especially in winter, and the earlier they learn to dress themselves for outdoors the better. So the best thing you can do, however much you enjoy their dependence on you, is to encourage them to zip up their own anoraks and fasten their own shoes. Three-year-olds should be capable of doing this. It may take them a little longer, but at least you probably don't have to teach them to tie their shoe-laces. Thank God for Velcro.

If you are taking more than one young child out, I strongly recommend enlisting the help of another grown-up; grandpa, perhaps. One to one is a good child to adult ratio. If you are on your own, just when you think you are being a really cool granny, all hell can break loose without warning. The toddler in the buggy starts to howl; the buggy starts to tip over from the weight of the shopping bags slung on the handles; the six-year-old starts to drag you by the hand towards the ice-cream van; and you desperately need to steer the dog into the gutter because you can see what he's about to do. Just don't expect a sympathy vote from passers-by. You are not the cool granny you thought you were. Nobody

is thinking 'What an attractive granny with her delightful, high-spirited grandchildren – she looks young
enough to be their mother.' You are blocking the pavement, and the only response your winsomely apologetic
smile will get is a stony stare. They
are thinking, 'Why doesn't that
stupid woman control those
children and get out
of my way?'

By car

If you have a car, your outings can take you further
afield. But you have to have a car seat. Without one, it is
illegal to drive a baby anywhere, even to the hospital in a
crisis. You can always transfer the car seat from the parents' car, but it's probably worth getting one of your
own. Familiarise yourself with it well in advance, making
sure you know how to install it in your car, and how to
strap the baby into it. It is by no means obvious. The fas-
tenings on car seats come second only to folding buggies

as objects designed to frustrate grannies and make them seem like complete idiots.

Most modern cars are fitted with special child-proof locks on the doors. Make sure these are activated before you put a child in the back seat; it is really dangerous to allow children in a car without them. I know of one two-year-old who opened the car door on the motorway. By great good luck the car was in a traffic jam and almost stationary.

You also need the backpack, a box of tissues and sweets, biscuits or raisins or other permitted snacks. In-car entertainment is optional but desirable. It can be in the form of tapes or CDs of nursery songs or other music familiar to the child. Or you can provide the musical entertainment yourself, if you are that way inclined.

My grandmother used to drive along country lanes with my brother and me squashed up beside her in the front seat, before seat belts were invented. She would sing and conduct, with both hands off the steering wheel (there was virtually no traffic in the 1940s), making up songs as she drove, usually about her neighbours:

> *Oh Mr Shaw Mellor, he is a good feller,*
> *His face is so yeller, he plays on the cello*
> *He's such a good feller, is Mr Shaw Mellor.*

We thought it was incredibly witty. One of the delights of spending time alone with your grandchildren is the license to be foolish. It may be this memory that prompts me to burst into song when I have grandchildren in the car. If only I could sing in tune. When my grandson Oscar was two, my off-key rendition of 'Baa baa black sheep' was greeted with the plea 'Don't sing, Granny Jane,' so now I try to contain my joie de vivre until my passenger has fallen asleep.

Sometimes the car is also the setting for serious conversations. Questions we as grandparents have had to field, apart, of course, from 'Are we nearly there?' include 'How long is an anaconda?' 'Who is God?' and 'What is poo made of?' If considering such matters at the same time as driving is too heavy a multi-tasking load, here are a few games to distract the budding scientists and philosophers.

Car games

• *I spy*, which you will not have forgotten how to play.

• *Guess the animal*: one person thinks of an animal and the others ask questions until they guess it. e.g. How many legs? Fur or feathers?

- **Red Dragon:** every time they spot a letter box they shout 'Red Dragon'. The person who shouts first wins a point.

- **Legs and arms** (for older children): on pub signs you score points for legs (e.g. plus 6 for Dog and Duck) and lose points for arms (minus 2 for King's Arms). Arguments break out about how many legs are allowed for the Coach and Horses.

- **Not finishing a word** (for older children): each person in turn says a letter, the object is not to spell a complete word, e.g. 'c, r, u, s', and if the next person says 't' he loses a point. It is a maddening game.

- **Number plate anagrams:** choose a number plate on another car, and then it is the first person to make a word using the letters in the right order. So if the letters on the plate are PHP, you might say 'PERHAPS'.

From the age of five or six, my grandchildren have enjoyed map reading. They may not be much good at it, but it is good training for the future. When our destination is a tourist attraction with a website, I download the map showing how to get there, printing a copy for each child. Otherwise we make do with a road atlas. When they are not studying the map, they are looking out for signposts, and 'Are we on the A420 yet?' is a slight improvement on 'Are we nearly there?'

When you reach your destination you will probably need the buggy. You will get it out and try to unfold it. But you will find you can't master it, in spite of the demonstration and practice you had before leaving home. It is not just you. All grandparents, virtually without exception, have this trouble. The folding pushchair is the one piece of modern equipment which utterly defeats them. They can neither open it up when they take it out of the car, nor collapse it when it is time to put it back. Most of us need more than one lesson followed by several practice goes at it. Even then, we'll probably have forgotten a week later. I intend to write down how it's done, and sketch a diagram, and keep it in the car. I shall also mark with red nail varnish the lever you have to push or pull.

Whatever you do, don't let the children out of the car before you have unfolded the buggy. It is an absolute nightmare wrestling with a buggy on the pavement or in a car park, putting your head back in the car to reassure the baby and trying to restrain a determined toddler, all at the same time. Luckily, in most public places, sooner or later a kind parent will take pity on you and show you what to do.

Not all routes you travel will be buggy-friendly. My grandson Max's school is only five minutes walk from his house, but to get there you have to cross a railway: twenty steps up, then across the bridge and another twenty steps down the other side. But it has never been a problem; every time I have had to negotiate the steps with his small brother in the buggy, a friendly helping hand has appeared.

By public transport

'You're a very useful engine, Thomas,' said the Fat Controller.

Standing on the railway platform, looking down the empty line, a toddler sees in his mind's eye Thomas pulling Annie and Clarabel, or Gordon pulling the express, or Percy shunting trucks. The toddler's granny sees in her mind's eye the opening scene from *Anna Karenina*, grabs the hood of his anorak and holds it tight. Thank goodness for the yellow line you must not cross, which didn't exist when we were children.

In those days, trains really were like Thomas, Edward, Henry, James and Gordon. Steam came out of their funnels, you could see the signal go down, and the coaches running along the track went 'diddle-i-dum, diddle-i-dum'. The hard-boiled egg smell of the second-class compartments (unaccountably known as 'third-class' — there was no second class) made you feel queasy, and the plush seats made your legs itch. If there was time, my brothers always wanted to go to the front of the train to see the engine before the journey. I was not interested. Terrified of being left behind, I just wanted to get aboard.

Is it politically incorrect to suggest that trains are a boy thing? It seems indisputably true. Show me a little girl with Thomas the Tank Engine pyjamas, Thomas toothbrushes, Thomas aprons, Thomas lunchboxes. It seems *de rigueur* for boys to have all these, and their idea of a great day out is to watch any train at any station. You may get bored standing waiting for a train to go by but your grandson never will. For a real treat, an outing to see 'the real Thomas' is hard to beat. We found him in the Forest of Dean in Gloucestershire. To get to him we had to run the gamut of gift shops and junk food stalls, but it was worth it; the Fat Controller was even in attendance.

Even if Thomas himself is not on parade, a trip on any steam train is a big attraction. There are a surprisingly large number of functioning steam railways up and down the country. For information about steam trains and railway museums, look at UK Heritage Railways' website:

ukhrail.uel.ac.uk. They can get very crowded during the holidays, at half-term and at weekends, so if you find crowds oppressive and are fearful of losing a grandchild in the mêlée, try and go midweek.

If you live in a city with an underground or metro, you can even turn shopping for the groceries into a treat. Instead of visiting your nearest shopping centre on foot, try travelling a couple of stops down the line to visit a different set of shops. Choose a time of day outside the rush hours. You need all the space you can get. I am sometimes shocked to see parents being indulgent to their children on public transport to the point where they become a nuisance to other passengers. I have seen children climbing over the seats with grubby shoes, grasping handrails with sticky fingers, and being generally noisy and obnoxious. I have seen others sitting quietly and behaving impeccably, so I know the unruly ones are the exception, and I'm sure that, in most cases, when granny is in charge they are not allowed to get away with it.

In crowded trains, I don't think children should necessarily have a seat to themselves. Recently I was on a full London tube train when two women with a little boy of two or three got on. Granny was holding the boy's hand, and the mother was holding a folded buggy. When a young man got up to offer his seat to the older woman (rare enough occurrence; full marks to him), the little boy immediately clambered on to it. 'Don't you want to sit on Nana's lap?' 'No.' For the rest of the journey the two women stood (as did several other elderly women) while the child sprawled on the seat. Have we become completely enslaved by our children and grandchildren?

For a serious journey, when you have to catch a specific train, for your own peace of mind and the children's, leave masses of time for getting to the station. Children can get just as agitated as grown-ups about catching a train, or more so. Nothing is so infectious as panic, and if you think you are cutting it too fine, your anxiety will communicate itself to your grandchild.

My mother instilled in me a life-long fear of missing trains by invariably living dangerously in this respect. 'Paddington Station, and drive like Jehu,' she would yell at the cab driver, flinging our baggage and herself into the back seat and dragging us in behind her. Now I can only feel calm if I am at the station a good half hour before my train goes, and I have been known to catch the train before the one I intended to travel on. There is plenty to do and see at a station or airport, and it is better to have time to kill than to be a nervous wreck.

On short journeys of half an hour or less, just being on the train provides enough amusement for most children.

On longer trips, you will need to provide additional entertainment. Looking out of the window to spot cows, sheep and horses or other trains in sidings helps to pass the time, and you can play some of the games you would play in the car. But it is just as well to have with you colouring books and crayons to bring out with a flourish when boredom sets in, a book to read and drinks and snacks to be doled out at intervals. Take the snacks with you, as you cannot leave a small child alone while you head off to the buffet car. When on a stopping train, I draw a chart showing the various stations, and we cross each one off as we arrive at it.

In most respects, a journey by bus with children is not very different from a journey by train, or even plane. Most of the advice given above applies equally to bus travel. I would caution against taking a child who suffers

from car sickness on a bus journey, against attempting it in rush hour, and against taking a buggy on a bus unless you are very confident and deft at folding and unfolding it. If you don't need the buggy, most children love a ride on a bus, especially if they can travel on the top deck of a double-decker. Let your grandchild press the button to tell the driver you want to get off at the next stop.

PART II – WHAT SHALL WE DO TODAY?

CHAPTER 6 – WHAT SHALL WE DO OUTSIDE?

In the country

Johnny Town Mouse: *It sounds rather a dull place?*
What do you do when it rains?
Timmy Willie: *When it rains I sit in my little sandy*
burrow and shell corn and seeds from my Autumn store.
I peep out at the throstles and blackbirds on the lawn,
and my friend Cock Robin. And when the sun comes out
again you should see my garden and the flowers — roses
and pinks and pansies — no noise except the birds and
bees, and the lambs in the meadow.

> *Johnny Town Mouse*, Beatrix Potter.

Children brought up in the country have enviable access to fields, hedgerows and woods. Their knowledge, not taught but absorbed, encompasses the names and habits of domestic and wild animals, birds and butterflies: where they live and what they eat. As they get older, country children get to know even quite complicatedly named wild flowers – cranesbill, ragged robin or scabious – and recognise the caterpillars of the Red Admiral or the Mullein moth. They know how to strip a hazel or chestnut leaf down to a fishbone skeleton, and tell the time with a dandelion clock. They learn to dam streams, play pooh-sticks, and catch tiddlers in ponds. They are unlikely to come to grief climbing a tree; children know their own limitations instinctively.

When we were children we spent happy summer hours in our grandparents' garden in Wiltshire sprawled on our tummies looking in the grass sward for four-leaved clovers, and watching ants and beetles go about their business, and trying to catch blackbirds and thrushes by putting salt on their tails. If you live in the country you can make all this available to city-dwelling grandchildren when they come to stay. They are never too young to start.

One of the great innovations since our days is the cross-country baby buggy – designed to cover rough terrain, and keep the baby safe and comfortable inside, it means, wherever you go, whether it is a Scottish moor, the Cornish coastal path, or a muddy farm, nobody has to stay at home to look after the baby. The baby comes too.

MUMS SAY:
I remember with my grandparents learning about wild flowers and animals, how to cut peat, and how to care for bees.

Grandma took us on lots of walks – I now love walking.

GRANNIES SAY:
We go on lots of walks and outings. I feel quite exhausted at the thought of it! Hunting things, races, hide and seek.

We go out and about a lot: hunting for hens' nests, logging, bonfires, feeding animals, picking flowers, preparing veg., walking in the woods.

Grannies, specially those who live in the country, put 'going for walks' high on their list of enjoyable activities with their grandchildren. But to some children the idea of going for a walk is anathema. 'It's boring.'

If, instead of saying, 'Would you like to go for a walk?' you say, 'Shall we go to the wild woods?' or 'Shall we go hunting?' or 'Shall we pick blackberries?' the response is much more enthusiastic. The interest in hunting may have been fostered by reading and watching stories about cave men, Cowboys and Indians, or Robin Hood and his Merry Men. I like to think it is a natural instinct. The way that boys pick up sticks and make believe they are guns, swords, or other weapons is another, less attractive manifestation of the same instinct. They just do it, however much one wishes they didn't.

But aggression is only a small part of the hunting experience. The children are quite philosophical if they never even see any prey, let alone get a chance to fire an arrow from their bows, or a pebble from their catapults. It is amazing how patient children who are normally restless can be when waiting for a rabbit to appear from its burrow, or a fish to bite the worm on the bent pin.

> *We're going on a bear hunt*
> *We're going to catch a big one*
> *We're not scared*
>> *We're Going on a Bear Hunt,*

The fun of hunting is in spotting the birds and animals, tracking them and stalking them: invariably unsuccessfully, but children are eternally optimistic. My grandfather offered £100 to any of his grandchildren who could kill a bird or a rabbit with a bow and arrow (making these is now one of my specialities — see instructions overleaf), and, in many years of school holidays none of us could claim it. But it was not for want of trying. We absorbed knowledge effortlessly, and now our own grandchildren are doing the same. They know which birds are pigeons (legitimate prey because you can eat them), and which are blackbirds (songbirds and you don't eat them although once upon a time they made a dainty dish to set before the king).

To 9ramy   Love Oscar

Indeed, this I think is another important way in which being a grandparent differs from being a parent. I don't

A Bow.

diameter about 1/2inch

1. Cut a straight stick 24 inches to 36 inches long, depending on the size of the child. Hazel wood is best

(only grown-ups can do this)

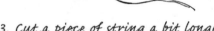

2. With a small sharp knife make a notch for the string, at each end of the bow.

3. Cut a piece of string a bit longer than the bow. Tie a loop in one end.

4. Attach the string to one end of the bow.

5. Hold the bow vertically, one end resting on the ground and bend it.

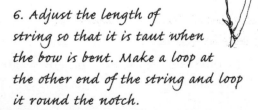

6. Adjust the length of string so that it is taut when the bow is bent. Make a loop at the other end of the string and loop it round the notch.

Arrows

1. Find some thin bamboo garden canes. Cut them to about 20 inches long.

2. Collect feathers (pigeon's or other) in the garden or a field.

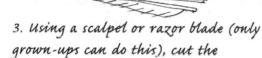

3. Using a scalpel or razor blade (only grown-ups can do this), cut the feathers' "stalk" in two lengthways.

4. With the blade or scissors, cut each 1/2 feather into 2 inch sections.

5. With blade or scissors, trim off 1inch of feathers.

6. With sticky tape or masking tape, bind 3 feather pieces to one end of the arrow, equally spaced apart.

7. For a really lethal weapon, sharpen the point and dip it in "poison".

remember repeating my own childhood in these ways with my children, but I get enormous pleasure from doing with my grandchildren the things my brothers and I did, all those years ago: squatting in the dust trying to coax a caterpillar to nibble a hazel leaf, racing big Roman snails, or tasting hawthorn haws. We called the haws 'bread and cheese' and I now read that they are rich in Vitamin C. The young leaves are edible too, although we did not know that.

> *Here we go gathering nuts in May*
> *On a cold and frosty morning.*

If some children have an instinctive urge to hunt, others seem to have an instinct for collecting. Am I allowed to speculate that often it seems to be the boys who hunt and the girls who gather? When you go for a walk you need capacious pockets or some kind of bag for their finds, which may include leaves, seedpods, fir-cones, conkers, acorns, snail shells, feathers and pebbles. In some parts of the country if you leave no stone unturned, sooner or later you will find a fossil or an Ancient Briton's flint arrowhead. Even more rare and exciting finds are fragments of animals' skeletons: skull of a weasel or a rabbit perhaps.

Fragments of sheep's wool can be collected, washed

and used to stuff a small soft toy or pincushion, or spun into thread. Feathers can be brought home to make Indian headdresses or to flight arrows with. And at the right time of year elderflowers can be picked to make cordial, and blackberries and mushrooms gathered — cook and eat the spoils when you get home. You don't need me to tell you, when you spot something interesting, to tactfully make sure your grandchild finds it before you do. Some finds can be used for art and craft projects, and others kept in a special box as part of a developing collection, to be converted, as the children get older, into a mini-museum. Decorating the box can be a satisfying project in itself.

Children also enjoy going to the local pick-your-own, especially when strawberries are in season. Each child should have her own little basket, bowl or punnet. Don't be too strict when fruit goes into the mouth rather than the punnet, and encourage the smallest and slowest pickers by dropping some of your own fruit into their container.

Johnny town mouse: *What is that fearful noise?*
(He started violently.)
Timmy Willie: *That? That is only a cow; I will beg
a little milk, they are quite harmless, unless they
happen to lie down on you.*
Johnny Town Mouse, Beatrix Potter

If your grandchildren are town mice, you may need to
introduce them gently to life in the country. They have
almost certainly got picture books telling them which
animals say 'moo' and which 'baa baa', but books cannot
convey the immense size of a cow, or the clamorous,
weighty urgency of a pig at feeding time. So be sympathetic to nervous children, allow them to hold your hand
tight and to hide behind you, lift them up and carry them
if necessary, and don't force them to go closer than they
want. They need time to develop confidence with unfamiliar creatures in unfamiliar surroundings.

Children like feeding ponies and horses, as long as
they are the other side of the gate or fence, so take
apples or carrots in your pocket. You need plenty, as
the children will drop them out of reach in a nettle
patch before the pony can reach them.

Some grown-ups are as scared as children about crossing a field full of cows, especially if they have a dog with
them (on a lead of course). Why are the cows putting

their heads down and looking so threatening? Are they about to stampede? Can I get the buggy and the toddler through that barbed wire fence quick enough if the worst comes to the worst? Be reassured. It is a well-known fact that cows are short-sighted. They have seen you moving out of the corner of their eyes, and that is why they put their heads down and forwards to get a closer look. Some of them may amble over to satisfy their curiosity. If they get too close for comfort, all you need do is wave your arms about and shout at them, and they will retire to a safe distance.

At the seaside

> Whenever a good nor'-wester blows,
> Christopher is certain of sand between the toes.
> A.A. Milne

Two of our grandchildren live within easy reach of the sea, and a trip to the beach is one of the outings we most enjoy. We much prefer to go out of season. The amusement arcades are closed and there is no queuing at the ice-cream stall or at the café, where on the coldest days, you can get hot chocolate and home-made cake. Children really don't care what the weather is like provided they are suitably dressed, and in the summer when the beach is crowded with other children it is only too easy to lose sight of yours.

I am neurotic about this because I once lost one of my children on a crowded beach, and although in those days we didn't imagine a paedophile round every corner as one has to now, it was a traumatic experience. I worked my way up and down the beach asking everyone, 'Have you seen a blonde four-year-old boy in a red Marks and Spencer T-shirt?' After twenty terrible minutes I spotted him jumping on someone else's sandcastle.

So, the emptier the beach, the better. There is also more space to play football and French cricket without getting in other people's way. If the tide is coming in we lose no time in getting digging, so we can throw up an impressive castle in time for the children to stand on it when the sea fills its moat.

As a mother I don't remember wanting to get involved with digging sandcastles. I was working on my suntan and hoping to get a few chapters of the latest blockbuster under my belt. It was the fathers who were supposed to bond with their children on the beach. The mothers adjusted the windbreak, minded the babies and tried to keep the sand out of the sandwiches and the dog away from other families' picnics.

Now, as a granny, I am very happy to do my share of

the digging, to help the little one make turrets in a bucket and knock them over, and to find shells to decorate the look-out towers. I can show the children how to make a sand-boat as a change from castles, and how to bury my legs.

She sells seashells on the sea shore.
The shells she sells are surely seashells.
So if she sells seashells on the sea shore,
I'm sure she sells seashore shells.

There is plenty to interest the hunter-gatherer on the right kind of beach, by which I mean one well-endowed with rocks encrusted with mussels and limpets, and rock pools where anemones and blennies, prawns and tiny crabs can be studied and pursued. The collector will follow the tide line or paddle in the shallows, picking up shells, driftwood, pebbles, and seaweed to take home as treasures. Babies love to have their legs dangled in the sea, and then be snatched away when a wave comes, and toddlers never tire of daring the tide like King Canute, then scampering up the beach when the water laps around their feet. What is more, a good blast of sea air is guaranteed to give everyone a sound night's sleep.

In the town

> *Timmy Willie, who had lived all his life in a garden, was almost frightened to death. There was no quiet; there seemed to be hundreds of carts passing; dogs barking; boys whistled in the street... The food disagreed with him; the noise prevented him sleeping.*
> *Johnnie Town Mouse*, Beatrix Potter

The whole world these days seems to be child-oriented in a way that it never was when we were bringing up our families. In most towns there is an embarrassment of choice of activities and projects. Museums often have special interactive (another word new to us in this context) projects to entertain children; some local sports and leisure centres are equipped for pre-school play; and most libraries have a children's corner where you can spend an hour or so looking at books and reading to your grandchildren. On certain days some have 'Story Time', with further entertainment laid on. Then there are seasonal events like Easter egg hunts, summer fêtes and Guy Fawkes bonfires.

Pottery painting centres are a relatively new concept, expensive but popular with grown-ups and children. You are given a plain plate, mug, jug or other piece, and a selection of colours, brushes and sponges with which to decorate your pottery. When you have finished, you leave it to be fired and collect it later. It makes a good outing if the children want to make a present for their parents. Even babies can participate, with your help, by making a hand or footprint on a plate.

When planning where to go and what to do, there is no need to cast yourself in the role of Saint Granny the Blessed Martyr. The children will have more fun if you are having fun too, so choose what *you* enjoy. But do also be aware that you may enjoy doing something you wouldn't normally dream of doing, like going swimming, or to the steam museum. The local newspaper, the ads in your newsagent's window or the notice board at the library will show you what entertainment is available. Useful headings to look under in Yellow Pages include 'Adventure and Activity Centres – children's' and 'Leisure Centres.'

Children love visiting indoor soft-play centres, a facility you may not have encountered. They are large open spaces, for example a warehouse, equipped with such apparatus as slides, giant foam rubber building blocks and huge balls. There is usually a café and sometimes a restaurant.

GRANNIES SAY:
They say they love being with me because we 'do' things – go to parks, the zoo, etc. It's much easier for a single granny as one devotes all the time to them.

Swimming is one of my favourite activities when I have just one grandchild to look after.

If your grandchildren are with you for just a week or less, one special day out is probably enough. However well it goes, you will all be worn out at the end of the day. The rest of their stay can be spent in low-key activities, such as a visit to the park or just going shopping with you.

Going to the park

> *Go down to Kew in lilac time, in lilac time, in lilac time;*
> *Go down to Kew in lilac time (it isn't far from London!)*
> *And you shall wander hand in hand with love in summer's*
>   *wonderland.*
>
> *Go down to Kew in lilac time (it isn't far from London!)*
>   Alfred Noyes

In many ways a walk in a city park is as much fun as a walk in the country. There are the same opportunities for finding treasures to bring home. If you are ambitious, it might be frogspawn or tadpoles in a jam jar. But more ordinary objects like snail shells, feathers or pretty pebbles also have their appeal, and can be used for crafts later.

Town-dwelling children love the chance to let off steam in an open space, and enjoy just running and jumping, especially if you join in. For homesick country bumpkins, accustomed to running free at home, the space is even more delightful. It is always worth taking a football for the children to practise their kicking and catching skills, but you must be prepared to join in.

If your park has a lake or pond, take some bread to feed the ducks, not too stale and certainly not mouldy as children invariably eat most of it themselves. It is considered irresponsible to feed pigeons, Canada geese or squirrels, as they have all become a serious menace, and their presence in the park should not be encouraged.

Hide and seek ranks high on grannies' lists of preferred activities, but can be rather nerve-racking in view of the golden rule that you should never let a child you are responsible for out of your sight. Luckily most toddlers think the whole point of the game is to be found immediately, and will rush out from their hiding place behind a tree before you have counted to ten.

If your grandchild is the proud owner of a scooter or tricycle, he is certain to want to take it to the park. If your journey to the park is on foot and your route involves crossing roads, I would persuade him to leave it behind, particularly if you are taking more than one child. Your heart will be in your mouth as the child on the scooter vanishes into the distance while you try in vain to run after it with a baby on your hip and one hand on the pushchair, your warning cries carried away on the wind.

The playground in the park may be the main attraction. Here, your town grandchild, who was timid and clumsy climbing trees with his country cousin, excels. He can shin up a climbing frame to dizzying heights, leaving the intrepid tree-climber hesitating below. In uncertain weather the Good Granny goes to the playground equipped with an old towel to dry off the slide and the swing seats. If you forget the towel you can sacrifice the spare nappy you brought along.

'Just one more jump, Roo, dear.' Like Kanga in *Winnie the Pooh*, you may find it difficult to drag your grandchild away from the slide or the swing in the playground, but try and quit while you're ahead, and leave them wanting more, even if it means offering a bribe such as an ice-cream on the way home, or a video to watch after tea. The main objective is to get them home before they are so tired you have to carry them.

If you are a keen gardener or a nature lover, a trip to the park is an opportunity to encourage your grandchild to share your love of flowers, trees, birds and butterflies. Naming names sometimes seems like a tedious waste of time, but keep at it. Repeated by you, over and over and over, it is remarkable how many are eventually retained in that developing memory.

Shopping with Granny

To market to market to buy a fat pig,
Home again, home again, dancing a jig.

On days when no special outings are planned, the children will enjoy joining in your ordinary routine, simply because it is different from the routine at home.

You can make your grandchild feel grown-up and special by asking him to help you make a shopping list before you leave home, and giving him a basket of his own to bring some of the shopping home in. My two-year-old grandson (a town mouse) chants a mantra every time he leaves the house – learnt, I presume, from his mother: 'Just getting my handbag, granny.'

If you normally do all your shopping in a supermarket, there is not much point in doing anything different just because your grandchild is with you – though, as you will know from observing other people's children in the aisles, there is nothing like a supermarket for encouraging bad behaviour. Try distracting her – before she gets a chance to start grabbing things that she wants but you don't – by enlisting her help. Ask her to show you where the vegetables are (although you already know this perfectly well) and get her to take things from the shelves that you do want, and put them in the trolley.

A trawl through the supermarket is less fun than a round trip taking in the butcher, the baker, the greengrocer and finally, as a reward for being good, the café or the sweet shop. A fishmonger, is, for some children, the most fascinating shop of all, but alas they are a dying breed.

The tricky part of the shopping trip comes when your grandchild spots something she wants, 'Will you buy me…' or even, 'Please, granny, will you buy me…' requires an instant answer. If the desired object is something unsuitable or trashy like a replica Kalashnikov or a sequinned boob tube, you will probably answer 'no,' and you will have to stick to your decision or lose face. Even if your grandchild wants to buy the disgusting object with her own pocket money, you may be tempted to dissuade her, on the grounds that her parents would not allow it.

Your hidden agenda here is that you don't want the parents to think your taste is so terrible that you approved the purchase, or that you are so feeble that you were bullied into agreeing to it. But what if the object of desire is a beautifully designed educational toy? Or perhaps a book? One still feels reluctant to be treated like a golden goose, and would prefer to choose and give presents on one's own terms. Your grandchild's perception of the world may already be more materialistic than yours, and she may live by a system of bribes and rewards that you don't wish to reinforce. Stick to your guns.

A GRANNY SAYS:
I love them dearly but sometimes they are very greedy and it annoys and upsets me when they keep asking me to buy them things.

Time your shopping expeditions to avoid the busiest times, so that you don't have to queue at the check-out, and the butcher, the baker and the greengrocer have time to chat and to admire your grandchild. And allow yourself time to wander home pausing to look at motorcycles parked by the roadside, building sites where you can see cranes and diggers at work, and any other local attractions offering free entertainment. If your route takes you along the river or canal, past a railway line or the fire station, better still.

CHAPTER 7 – WHAT SHALL WE DO AT HOME?

It may not always suit you to take your grandchildren out for trips and treats. You may be waiting in for a delivery, or a telephone call. It may be a case of: 'The North wind doth blow, and we shall have snow.' Or you may have exhausted the children rushing about in the park the day before. You can have an equally happy time indoors. Don't think you have to play with them all the time. Leave them to get on with their own games for as long as they remain absorbed and happy, for non-stop interaction is tiring for the children as well as for you.

Although much of this book is about activities that you and your grandchildren can enjoy together, the time you spend talking, and, perhaps more important, listening, is sometimes the most appreciated of all. When life is so hectic that communication at home is reduced to 'Don't forget to brush your teeth', 'Your P.E. kit is in the drier', 'It's orchestra today, so make sure you take your cello' – a leisurely conversation, or even a companionable silence, is a pleasurable luxury for the child. The important thing is to be together, and not to be in a hurry. I can hardly repeat too often that, unlike parents, grandparents are supposed to have all the time in the world.

MUMS SAY:

Because my gran and I were so close we could spend time doing not very much, or just pottering about in the garden or chatting for a few minutes.

My grandmother was always a comforting presence and a good listener.

My grandma spent lots of time talking to us and asking questions about school, friends, etc. and was very interested in our replies.

With my parents my boys have enjoyed: making jam, picking fruit and veg. from the garden, searching for fossils on the beach, learning to sew,

making bread… All things they've never done at home.

She was an absolutely brilliant grandmother, we stayed with her a lot and she taught us loads of card games and how to knit and crochet. She also taught us rude words to songs.

My granny was the best… baking, art, picnics… you name it she did it.

My mum spends hours playing with my daughter pretending to be her baby or something just as silly.

I particularly associate drawing and painting with my granny. When we arrived to stay, the playroom table would be laid out very neatly, with freshly sharpened pencils, little piles of paper, and sausages of plasticine ready for moulding.

GRANNIES SAY:
Singing and reciting Hilaire Belloc poems are popular; my grandchildren are getting better at cards, and I am on firmer ground than when playing rugby or football.

We tend to play card games or snakes and ladders.

We play chess. The children are only 8, 6 and 6. Aren't they brilliant?

We play silly games like HOW TO MARRY A DUKE (walking about with a book on your head). And anything with cardboard boxes.

The Umpire's decision is final and I am the Umpire.

We pretend to be dinosaurs.

We do puzzles, drawing, cooking, play-dough, and play snap, junior scrabble, the memory game, etc.

They love it when grandpa makes coins disappear then finds them behind their ear.

We let them be, to entertain themselves most of the time.

One time we redesigned and painted the small bedroom with all four walls painted and designed by a different child, with new curtains and lampshades to blend in.

This little piggy

Babies under six months love lots of attention. If you are busy you can have the baby by you in his bouncy seat on the kitchen table, or lying on the floor in his 'gym' (a splendid new concept). Just chatting away to him and coming within smiling range every now and then will keep a baby happy for a while. Their reactions are slower than ours, so when you are interacting with a baby, don't turn away before he has had time to respond.

A MUM SAYS:
I love my mum's ability to simply play with the baby, without apparently wanting to do anything else.

With your first grandchild the games you used to play with your own children will come flooding back, and you will automatically slip into playing Peek-a-boo or Peep-bo. 'Round and round the garden like a teddy bear' is another classic hit with the smallest babies.

From nine months on, they chortle hysterically in games where you bounce them up and down on your knee, as in 'This is the way the farmers ride' and 'Row, row, row the boat'. You can make up your own chants to go with knee rides. It is a grandfather's privilege to work a child up into an hysterical frenzy with this kind of game, then hand him back to a parent or to granny.

At this age they are learning new skills all the time, becoming for example, adept at picking things up and moving them around. If you sit the baby on the floor with a box of household oddments she will happily take the things in and out of the box and push them around. They should be unbreakable, too large to swallow, and should not have sharp edges. Cotton reels, plastic cups and spoons, a tea strainer, a plastic dinosaur, all fit the bill. Toddlers also love just bringing you things then taking them away again.

Housework

Above all, children like to do what you do. Little ones love doing housework with you – but it does take ten times longer than doing it by yourself. Either you get bored long before they do, or on the contrary, their attention span is so short that they never finish a job. Either way, you can avoid getting frustrated if you just slow down your normal brisk pace, and go with their flow. Lower your (no doubt impeccably high) standards for the duration of their visit, or if you can't bear to do that, do the job again properly after they're in bed.

MUMS SAY:
I used to go and polish grandma's furniture sometimes.

The children really love spending time with their granny – she carries on with her daily tasks and they just help out.

Children are not as bored by routine chores as you are. They love to load and unload the washing machine, spin-dryer and dishwasher. A request to lay the table will all too soon be met by older children with 'Do I have to?' so make the most of the enthusiasm the little ones show for this job. Even if the results are a little bizarre, suspend your critical instincts and curb the urge to supervise more than is strictly necessary.

One of the most successful presents my co-granny gave our oldest grandson was a toy Hoover. It kept him happily occupied for hours on end. Strangely enough he was not interested in a toy dustpan and brush, but loved sweeping up with the real thing.

> *She looked so neat and nimble, O,*
> *A-washing of her linen, O.*

If you are doing a handwash let your grandchild have a bowl of soapsuds too, with lots of bubbles, to wash dolls clothes, or their own socks. When you unload the spin-dryer, he can help you sort the clothes, putting each item into 'Mummy's pile', 'Daddy's pile', 'my pile', and so on.

Toy irons are a success with some children but, as with the dustpan, my grandson won't be fooled. He spends happy hours ironing the carpet with a broken iron, an expression of total concentration on his face, while I am busy at the ironing board nearby. Naturally it is not plugged in and is only used at ground level so small fingers or toes are safe.

The kitchen sink

> *I'm forever blowing bubbles,*
> *Pretty bubbles in the air,*
> *They fly so high,*
> *Nearly reach the sky,*
> *Then like my dreams*
> *They fade and die.*

For children, the sink is not so much a washing-up station as an all-singing, all-dancing Lido complete with fountains and cascades. It seems children never tire of water play. If you want to get on with your own chores, put a pvc apron on your grandchild, pull a chair up to the sink and he will experiment happily until you decide he has had enough.

When you have more or less filled the sink with water of the right temperature (tepid), turn the hot tap off tightly so little fingers cannot turn it back on. Children find taps irresistible and, with access to the cold tap only, their hands will get cold after a while and you will have to top up with hot water again. A small amount of washing up liquid will produce some satisfactory bubbles, which can be whipped up with a balloon egg whisk. Provide an assortment of plastic jugs, mugs, bottles, colander and strainer and an empty washing-up-liquid bottle to squirt. Ping-pong balls and empty plastic squeezy lemons are fun because they float. As well as experimenting with all the fascinating things water can do, they might enjoy bathing their dolls, action men and dinosaurs. There will be a mess of water on the floor to mop up afterwards, and the children will probably need to change into dry clothes, but it will have bought you an hour or two of uninterrupted time.

When he was five, my grandson begged to do 'apple bobbing' after seeing it on television. After a failed experiment with a full washing-up bowl and some rather large Granny Smiths, we decided the bath would be a better place and smaller apples would give him a chance of success. In fine weather bowls of water can be put outdoors, as long as you are out there yourself, or they are in full view from the kitchen window. Make paper boats to play with.

Granny can we make a cake?

There are two ways of cooking with children: one is to let them 'help' you with routine cooking you would be

To make a paper boat:

1. Take an A4 sheet of paper.

2. Fold it in half.

3. Fold the top corners E and F to the centre.

4. Fold the flap A-B up. Turn over and do the same with flap C-D. Then open out from the centre and flatten into diamond shape.

 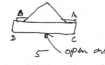 

5 & 6. Fold up the AB point as shown. turn over and fold up the CD point.

7 & 8 Put your fingers into the centre and pull the two pointed ends gently apart, at the same time folding both sides up, coaxing it into the shape of a boat.

9. Make lots more and organise a naval battle on a pond or in the bath.

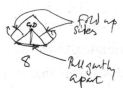

doing anyway. The other is to have a special cooking session for their benefit. (For more on cooking with children and recipe ideas, see *CHAPTER 9 – FOOD.*)

Play-dough

A third option is pretend cooking. Play-dough comes somewhere between cooking and artwork. It is edible, and will not harm a child, but the high salt content makes it unappetising. You can buy ready-made play-dough at toyshops, but it easy and fun for children to make, with some supervision. It is a wonderfully versatile substance. Children can learn as they play by weighing it out. It can be rolled out like pastry dough and cut into shapes for pretend biscuits and pies. Small bits of dough can be rolled into balls to make 'fruits' and patterns can be made in the dough by pressing a potato masher, a coin or a piece of coarsely-woven material into it.

When two or more children play together, avoid any fighting by making sure each has his own tools: same rolling pin, same cutters, same colour dough.

Play-dough will keep in a lidded plastic container for at least a year, and can be used again and again, so each grandchild can keep his own supply at your house. It is also better than the messier plasticine or clay for making models. Any model that can be made with clay can also

Definitive play-dough recipe

2 cups plain flour
1 cup salt
4 tablespoons of cream of tartar (sounds a lot, but you do need this much)
2 cups water
2 tablespoons cooking oil (e.g. sunflower oil)
food colouring

Mix the flour, salt and cream of tartar in a saucepan. Stir in the water, oil and colouring, till the mixture is smooth.

Cook over a low heat for 3 to 5 minutes, stirring all the time. Remove from heat and set aside to cool. It is ready to use as soon as it is cool enough to handle. Don't worry if the mixture is a bit lumpy, it will come smooth as you knead it.

be made with play-dough: animals, birds, snakes, dinosaurs, men, plates, mugs. Keep a collage box and bring it out to decorate models with feathers, bits of ribbon, buttons, pipe-cleaners, spent matches, pasta shapes. Unless they are clearly at a loss how to proceed, it is best not to offer children ideas about what to make. Let them use their imagination, and don't be disappointed if they don't make anything at all. Some children will happily spend hours just squidging the dough and pushing it about.

'Just going to the office, granny.'

Heigh ho! Heigh ho!
It's off to work we go.

'I let her play with everything I possess, pen and ink, paste pot, watch, specs, scissors, glue bottles, letter-receiver, Concordance, Bible and all!
Hanah Whitall Smith, *A Quaker Grandmother*, 1888

Just as children like to share housework with you, so, too, do they like to share your working life. Going to the office is probably what mummy and daddy do, so it's natural the children want to play at it too. Those of us who have an office at home are guardians of the gates of paradise.

The computer is rationed, but useful for learning to read and spell, and for printing off drawings of TV characters to colour in.

Having a go at the photocopier, telephone, or swivel chair are one-off treats, but there are lesser things to play with giving hours of pleasure: hole puncher, stapler, pencil sharpener, scissors (safety). Add masses of paper, pencils, marker pens, a ruler and a set square, and give your grandchild his own small table and chair in a corner of your office and he can play 'going to the office' to his heart's content. You may not get much work done, but at least he will be happily occupied for an hour or so.

Special treasures

Some grandparents have treasures that are brought out when grandchildren visit, and played with as a special treat.

> *'Grandmother let me look over the drawers where she kept her beautiful scraps of silk and velvet, ever so many of which she gave me... She let me 'tidy' her best work-box, a wonderful box full of every conceivable treasure and curiosity.'*
>
> Mrs Molesworth, *Grandmother Dear*, 1878

My grandmother had an antique clockwork musical box we were allowed to wind up. My mother had a collection of small ivory animals from India and her grandchildren loved playing 'hunt the elephant', her variation on 'hunt the thimble', and a granny of my own generation has a very beautiful and well-equipped doll's house which she inherited from her own grandmother. When her grandchildren visit the house is opened up and she and they play together with the little family who live there, moving the miniature furniture around and serving up the miniature leg of lamb, cakes and jellies.

Granny's little Leonardo

> '*Reeling and writing and fainting in coils*'
> Lewis Carroll

How have I got so far in this book without mentioning *Blue Peter*? *Blue Peter*, a shining example of the best of children's television, was so influential for my generation of mothers that I still cannot bring myself to throw away the cardboard inner tube from a roll of lavatory paper. Woe betide the mother who could not come up with a plastic bottle and some sticky-back plastic at Val's behest, in order to make an engine or a beautiful and useful present for a grandma, granddad or auntie. My daughter's *Blue Peter* repertoire included a shell-covered jewellery box; an advent crown made of coat-hangers covered in tinsel, complete with candles; and a boat made from a bottle with wooden skewers for masts.

If you and your grandchildren run out of ideas of your own for arts and crafts, some of today's children's TV programmes follow the trail blazed by *Blue Peter*, offering lots of ideas for different age groups. With younger children you will definitely need to be hands-on. A lot of the art ideas you think up will already be familiar to children of school age or those who go to a nursery. But they will have more fun doing them with you.

A child-sized easel earns its keep. They are available with a blackboard on one side and a magnetised sur-

face on the other, so that, with a packet of magnetised alphabet letters you can start teaching them to recognise their own and family names and a few simple words. A roll of lining paper from the D-I-Y shop is useful – children get through an awful lot of paper. For obvious reasons paints and felt-tips should be water-soluble, and vulnerable surfaces including your clothes and the children's should be protected.

The children will enjoy getting everything ready, covering the table, getting out the paints, filling water jars. If you need to buy paint or glue brushes, paper, glue or the ingredients for play-dough, make the shopping expedition part of the fun.

Eighteen months is not too young to start painting with hands and fingers or big brushes. I don't remember finger painting when I was a child, and I don't remember doing it with my children, but it is fun. Powder paint will go further if you mix it half and half with flour, then add water till, by trial and error, you get it to the right consistency.

A spoonful of washing-up liquid added to paint makes it easier to wash off when you have spills. You need large sheets or a roll of thick paper. The children can experiment at random, or you can show them how to make handprints and, if you like, footprints too.

For stencilling and printing, runny paint needs thickening with washing-up liquid or flour. Try cutting a crude pattern on the cut side of half a potato, or slicing fruit and vegetables which already have their own pattern. Peppers work well.

For painting cardboard models (and a model need only be a shoe box calling itself a train), you can get special effects by mixing sand with emulsion paint, or wallpaper glue with powder paints.

The paraphernalia of paints, brushes and pots of water can be time-consuming and messy to assemble and clear away; chunky felt pens with water-based, washable colours are an easier option. While your grandchild sits at the kitchen table with colours and scrap paper, you can get on with undemanding chores such as peeling potatoes or washing-up. If you forgot to get a colouring book,don't fret. You can download from the Internet pictures of your grandchild's favourite TV cartoons to colour in.

Your grandchild is not Picasso (truly, I promise you), so don't save the artwork for ever. Once it has delighted you for long enough, bin it. She will have forgotten all about it by next time. Having said that, 35 years on I still treasure the box with painted shells stuck on its lid by my daughter, together with a stone painted by my son to vaguely resemble a frog.

The Collage box

If you are a hoarder by nature, your moment has come at last. Nothing is too trivial to go in the art box. Buttons, beads, feathers, scraps of ribbon and fabric, lace, tinsel, leaves, pasta, beans, lentils, picture postcards, pictures cut from magazines and all those catalogues you never got round to chucking out. Children love cutting out and gluing things – indeed children love scissors altogether; if you don't watch out they will to give themselves or their siblings an interesting new hairstyle – and are drawn like little magpies to anything that glitters.

This glorious mish-mash of media can be used in all sorts of ways. Budding fashion designers can thread beads and stitch and glue scraps of fabric to dress their dolls and teddies. Boxes of different shapes and sizes (saved by the hoarder because they will 'come in useful'), plastic bottles and flowerpots, can all be decorated, the more extravagantly the better.

All these artefacts make splendid Christmas and birthday presents for parents and co-grandparents. Other seasonal goodies to make include Christmas cards, wrapping paper and gift tags, or Easter eggs.

Rudimentary origami

If you are bad granny and have not managed to assemble any arts and crafts kit, all is not lost. You have got yesterday's newspaper or the *Radio Times* or last months *Saga* magazine.

Introduce your grandchildren to paper darts, cut-out dancers, a fortune teller or a snake:

A Snake

1. Cut two thin strips of paper at least 30 cm long. They can be different colours.

stick together

2. Join them at one end, at right angles, with glue or sticky tape.

3. Fold each strip over the other alternately, till all the paper is used up.

a   b   c   d   e   etc etc

4. Draw a snake's head on the final fold.

5. Pull out from each end like a concertina.

Fortune Teller

1. Make a square of paper
by folding diagonally
and cutting off the surplus.

 2. To find the centre, fold
diagonally again, then unfold

 3. Fold each corner
to the centre.

 4. Turn over and fold corners to
centre again.

5. Fold in half and press the
fold to crease it. Unfold and
do the same long-ways.

6. Pull each corner out to make a pouch
for each forefinger and thumb.

7. Colour or number each of
the 8 inside flaps differently.

8. Open each flap and write the
'fortune' inside it.

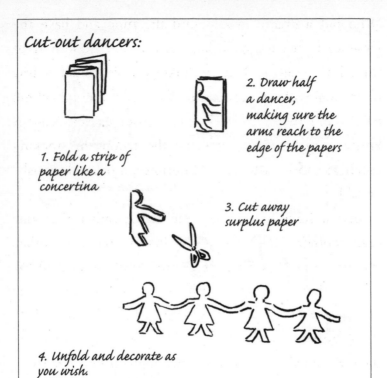

Cut-out dancers:

1. Fold a strip of paper like a concertina

2. Draw half a dancer, making sure the arms reach to the edge of the papers

3. Cut away surplus paper

4. Unfold and decorate as you wish.

k1, p1, k2tog

A GRANDCHILDREN SAYS:
My grandmother knitted for England. She had endless patience and taught me and my brother to sew, knit and crochet.

Who but a granny would find the time and have the patience to teach a child how to knit, let alone how to thread a needle to hem a hankie or embroider a tray cloth? Many of my generation of grannies were wartime babies and therefore we were surrounded by diligent knitters, making comforts for the troops in stocking stitch, rib, moss stitch and sometimes, most ambitiously, in cable.

In our household it was the aunts, rather than our grandmother who knitted, one in navy blue, the other two in khaki. They always had time to cast on or off for us, or to pick up dropped stitches. We would hunch over our work muttering, 'in, over, through, off,' making kettle-holders with chunky wool on knitting needles as thick as pencils, which gave satisfyingly instant results.

Our children were more ambitious, making Dr Who scarves with oddments of wool left over from granny's knitting (she averaged one garment per grandchild per year).

Our daughter made a scarf almost as long as the Doctor's and wore it with pride. Our son managed to knit an item of more modest dimensions: a striped collar for Rex, our unsatisfactory Labrador with wanderlust. Conversations with the local police would take place at frequent intervals:

'Our dog has gone missing, and I wonder if any-one has reported finding him? He's a pale golden labrador.'

'Is he wearing a name tag?'

(Apologetically) 'No, but he's wearing a striped, knitted collar.'

'We have him here, madam.'

During World War II nothing was ever wasted, and the habit dies hard. When a parcel came, the brown paper wrapping was smoothed out and folded away, to be used again and the smallest lengths of string were saved. Bits of string found their way into pockets and were brought out from time to time to play 'cat's cradle,' a skill, like riding a bicycle, that never quite leaves you, should you wish to pass it on the another generation. Oddments of wool left over from knitting were used to make multi-coloured pompoms to decorate a hat or scarf. We used to make them to hang above the latest baby cousin's pram or cot.

Can we fix it? Yes we can

A MUM SAYS:
My dad is not a natural hands-on with little children, but he has been brilliant at teaching them new skills, giving them new experiences, and making things.

For some children a miniature set of tools is a dream come true. Others will only use proper grown-up equipment. Bits of wood, nails and a hammer will keep them happy for hours. They can graduate to screws and a screwdriver if you drill the holes for them.

Some children are happy to let off steam just hammering. But with these basic tools, a few off-cuts of wood, and perhaps a little help, your grandchild can make a gun, boat, aeroplane or doll's bed. Only very rudimentary construction techniques are needed; the imagination does the rest.

'You *shall* go to the ball, Cinderella'

My grandmother kept a 'dressing-up box', a large old army trunk brought out for a very occasional and special rainy day treat, or to kit us out to perform a Christmas play or concert. In it were hats, including a gent's opera hat (a collapsible top-hat), scarves, a nurse's outfit, cowboy suit, Indian feather headdress, assorted oddments of clothing including waistcoats, velvet and silk skirts and tops, frilly petticoats, net curtains, moth-eaten fur tippets and a much-fought-over ostrich feather.

It is never too soon to start your own collection. Before you give anything to the charity shop or jumble sale, check out its dressing-up potential. Hats, high-heeled shoes, handbags and jewellery (bangles and beads, the gaudier the better) are very popular. Look in charity shops for suitably exotic garments. A hideous neon-pink lurex frock is fit for a princess in the eyes of a five-year-old. Have plenty of belts to hold up skirts and trousers that are inevitably several sizes too big. Useful props include toy swords and shields, crowns and tiaras.

Two or more children left to themselves will probably settle down to role-playing games with only the gentlest prompting, with or without dressing-up: playing shops with the aid of a few items of real or pretend merchandise and money, playing mummies and daddies to a family of dolls and teddies. When it comes to the game of doctors and nurses, prepare to be mildly shocked; children's natural curiosity about each other's bodies needs satisfying, and modern parents are probably more open and liberal than we were.

A GRANNY SAYS:
The two little cousins developed a taste for throwing off all their clothes and jumping into bed together under the duvet in the middle of the afternoon! We tried to dissuade gently and then to ignore, and they did seem to lose interest eventually, but it took time.

Once upon a time

You can probably remember some of the classic nursery stories well enough to tell them without prompting: the Three Little Pigs, Goldilocks and the Three Bears, or the Billy Goats Gruff. I would advise you to steer clear of Little Red Riding Hood – your grandchildren just might start looking anxiously at your teeth.

But children like it best if you invent a story especially for them. My grandmother used to tell one about an American GI called Leo the Lion who parked his chewing gum on the garden wall and had a friend called Fanny the Giraffe.

You can make up stories in which your grandchildren are the heroes, and they love to hear about terribly naughty children and, by way of contrast, insufferable goody-goodies. If your grandchild has an imaginary friend, respect his or her existence, and behave (within reason) as if he/she is real.

The enlightened re-writing of history has changed the focus of some traditional stories. In the Wild West, the Indians, who were for so long portrayed as the villains, destined always to bite the dust eventually, have now become the goodies, and the cowboys are revealed as baddies who stole their land and hunted their buffalo to extinction.

Pom-pom

1. Cut out two cardboard discs of the same size with a hole in the middle

2. Place them together and wind wool round and round and round. You will have to wind off balls of wool small enough to pass through the central hole, which gets smaller as you progress. The balls can be in one, two or more colours

3. The last part is tricky, and needs an adult. Using small, sharp scissors, cut the wool all round the outside edge

4. Slide a triple strand of wool between the two cardboard discs and tie it tightly with a knot

5. Ease the two discs away on each side and you are left with a ball, which just needs fluffing up

6. The triple strands of wool can be plaited to make a neat string to hang the ball

A much-loved story which I can still recite by heart was Helen Bannerman's marvellous *Story of Little Black Sambo*. It was banned from right-thinking nurseries for a generation because it was considered racist, but is now accepted again on the grounds that the eponymous hero is not an African but an Indian boy living in India, which makes the references to his colour no more racist than the references to the colour of Goldilocks' hair in The Story of the Three Bears.

One of the important functions of a grandparent, as touched on in *CHAPTER 1*, is that of family historian. Grandparents are in a unique position to look back and look forwards at the same time, connecting the past to the future. They are able to tell their grandchildren how it was when they were young, and describe their own parents and grandparents. I bitterly regret not having encouraged my grandparents to tell me about the past. Now it is too late, and I can never know. You have lived through interesting times, so try and make your stories about the old days lively, and keep at it, however bored your audience may seem. Some of it will sink in, and later they will be glad of it. Show them photographs. Describe the ludicrous clothes and hairstyles of your youth. Reminisce about the strange old-fashioned way of listening to music on your parents' wind-up gramophone. Sing them the songs you used to sing as a child. Tell them what you did before television was invented.

Indoor gardening

Children love planting things and sowing seeds. But the results must be quick or they will soon lose interest.

Seeds

Mustard and cress are fastest of all: from seed to sandwich in 11-14 days. Sow the seeds on several layers of wet kitchen paper on a plate or baking tray. Cress takes a few days longer than mustard, and should be sown first. Make sure the paper doesn't dry out. The easiest way to keep it damp without drowning the seedlings is to use a spray: the kind you use to dampen the clothes for ironing.

Variations on a mustard and cress theme include eggshells painted with faces and filled with damp cotton wool. Seeds sown on the cotton wool grow like hair on the egghead. You can also grow mustard and cress on potatoes. Poke holes in the potato with a cocktail stick and push the seed into the holes. Two or more potatoes can be joined together with sticks for legs to make hairy animals. There is no need to water the potatoes, they already contain enough moisture.

Beans, nasturtiums and sunflowers can also be sprouted on wet cotton wool or paper. When they are big enough you can plant them and grow them on, in small pots of compost. The method of growing a broad bean in a jam jar lined with blotting paper is tried and tested provided you don't allow the paper to dry out. Soak the bean in water for 24 hours then put it between the blotting paper and the jar. Soon roots and shoots will appear.

Pips saved from oranges, lemons, satsumas and grapefruits will germinate in damp potting compost. Soak the pips overnight and plant in small plastic flower pots (painting and decorating the pots can be part of the fun), several pips per pot. Put in a warm, dark place, spraying occasionally to keep the compost damp. When shoots appear, bring the pots into the light on a warm windowsill. Over the years the pip will become a small tree, but don't expect it to produce fruit unless it has a partner to pollinate it.

Vegetable tops

> Mary, Mary, quite contrary,
> How does your garden grow?
> With silver bells and cockle shells,
> And pretty maids all in a row.

This works with carrots, parsnips, beetroots, Swedes, turnips and the rather more exotic pineapple. If the vegetables have leaves, trim them back to 0.75cm ($^1/_4$ inch). Slice off their tops 1cm ($^1/_2$ inch) and put them cut-side down on a shallow dish with enough water to cover the base of the vegetables. Add more water if it dries out and after a few weeks the veg top will sprout new leaves. Just one is fun, but a mix of, say, carrot and beetroot, in a roasting tin or on a plastic tray, with pebbles scattered between them, makes a little garden. The *objets trouvés* from your last walk will come in handy: scraps of moss, shells, pebbles, twigs. A small mirror or a piece of foil makes a pond. The silver bells may be hard to come by, but the pretty maids all in a row can be paper cut-outs.

Bulbs

As with the broad bean, part of the fun is watching the roots grow. Balance a hyacinth or daffodil bulb on a narrow-necked glass jar full of water. A wine carafe is ideal. Keep the water topped up. A small piece of charcoal will keep it sweet. Bulbs need only water to grow and flower; all their other requirements are contained in their flesh. If you grow indoor bulbs, let the grandchildren help you plant up the pots.

Grandpa's tricks

I hope it will not be considered sexist if I remark on some minor differences between the skills, talents and inclinations of grandmothers and grandfathers. I dare say it is due to the way we were brought up, but it seems to me indisputable that men of our generation are better at carpentry than women, that women are better at sewing and knitting and, if not better at cooking, more accustomed to doing it, and that men are less demonstrative of their affection.

There is another difference that I notice when I see grandfathers with their grandchildren. They go in a great deal more for jokes, teases and conjuring tricks than grandmothers do. If I was writing this for grandpas, I would include instructions for a few tricks on the lines of a vanishing coin, or Spot the Lady. As it is, I will just show you how Grandpa's hanky mouse is made (see p207). It is a trick that has kept generations of children entranced.

Playing games

BT (Before Telly) families played games: card games like Snap, Strip-Jack-Naked (aka Beggar My Neighbour), Donkey, Whist, Happy Families and so on; board games like Snakes and Ladders, Lotto, L'Attaque, Monopoly, and the classics, Dominoes, Draughts and Chess. Both grannies and grandpas take pleasure in introducing another generation to the games of their own childhood, and the children seem to enjoy playing them.

There is a school of thought which says you should let them win when they are very small, to foster their enjoyment of the game, and build up their confidence. There is another school that says, with the Dodo in *Alice in Wonderland*, after the caucus race, 'All have won and all shall have prizes.' Or, put another way, 'The race is not to the swift, nor the battle to the strong' (*Ecclesiastes*, 9.11). If, as many parents and grandparents do, we see games as preparation for life, as well as entertainment, it is difficult to agree with the Dodo and the Prophet.

It is true, competitiveness is played down in some schools, and stars awarded for 'helping your friends' rather than for running faster than them, or being better at sums. The situation in other schools is different and more like the one that prevailed in our youth. In these schools, grannies waiting at the gates are likely to be greeted with 'Guess what, granny, I came second in spelling' or 'I got a Head Teacher's Award.'

Most grandparents will probably take a position somewhere between the two. They want their grandchildren to compete successfully when they are in a compet-

Grandpa's hanky mouse

1. Fold a hanky or napkin diagonally

2. Fold corners to middle

3. Roll up from the bottom

4. Flip the whole thing over

5. Fold into thirds

6. Turn both flaps up and
then turn the whole thing inside out

7. Find and gently pull out tail

With a little sleight of hand you can stroke the mouse and
make it seem to scamper up your arm and down your neck.

itive environment, but, if they are not high achievers, grandparents don't want them to lose confidence. In those circumstances, hearing the story of the Hare and the Tortoise from granny, and being allowed to beat her at Snap may work wonders.

In the end, we would like, by playing games with our grandchildren, to teach them to be good losers and graceful winners. This is easier said than done. I fear good losers are born, not made; but bad losers can at least learn not to let it show, and winners be taught not to crow.

The last resort

Inevitably, sooner or later, your grandchildren will ask to watch a favourite TV programme. We all pay lip-service to the principle that plonking a child in front of the TV should be a last resort, not a regular part of our routine – but is it really so wicked? There are plenty of educa-tional programmes, wildlife programmes and serialisa-tions of classic children's books, and what could be more delightful than to sit on the sofa watching them together? We will probably learn a lot of things we didn't know, too.

Alas it is not that simple. When our children were at the pre-school stage, *Watch with Mother* was restricted to a short period each day. Today children's TV is available almost non-stop from 6am until 7pm. However, an hour once in a while so that granny can nod off is not going to give them square eyes.

With a little low cunning you can select programmes you yourself enjoy, and reject the ugly, loud and garish ones. I'd settle for a *Blue Cow Story* and an occasional look at *Balamory* and I have finally come round to *Teletubbies* because the children love it so. But they don't make 'em like they used to. Oh Florence, oh Zebedee, where are you? Come back, *Magic Roundabout*. (It is just possible my prayer has been heard. A new *Magic Roundabout* film is in production as I write).

If your grandchild begs and begs and nags and nags to watch something that you know to be unsuitable or feel to be trashy, honesty is not always the best policy, and I don't mind occasionally lying to my grandchildren to avoid a battle.

When I don't want them to watch I might tell them the TV has broken down, I have lost the zapper, or only Grandpa knows how to switch it on. At one time or another I have used all these excuses to wean them off the drug, though I have to admit that on other occasions I behave more like a drug pusher.

GRANNIES SAY

I do think they watch too much television, but I'm sure we all use it as a desperate measure if one is busy or the weather is poor.

They watch far less TV in my house, plus I don't have computer games.

CHAPTER 8 – WHAT SHALL WE DO IN THE GARDEN?

'To own a bit of ground, to scratch it with a hoe, to plant seeds, and watch their renewal of life – this is the commonest delight of the race, the most satisfactory thing a man can do.'

Charles Dudley Warner

If gardens and gardening have ever meant anything to you, in life or in literature, you will want to pass that on to your grandchildren. Seeing them enjoy the colours, textures and scents of plants you have loved, will give you enormous satisfaction. And, if you can show them the magic of putting a dried up seed or a twig in the ground and tending it lovingly until it produces a plant with flowers and fruit, you will, with a bit of luck, have introduced them to a life-long pleasure.

Nostalgia is a strong influence on the way we garden. In our own garden I love growing the plants my grandmother grew in hers: delphiniums, Japanese anemones, lavender, lupins, phlox, Scotch thistle; and the bees and butterflies work them over here and now just as they did there and then. If I am still alive when my grandchildren have grown up and have gardens of their own, I will save seeds, take cuttings and dig up plants for them, and this will be one of the ways in which we will achieve continuity from generation to generation. Meanwhile I am making sure a few of my favourite flowers bloom in their parents' gardens.

All babies love flowers and will reach out and grab them if they can get within crawling or shuffling distance. If you want a child to love flowers, it seems mad to say 'No' every time she touches one, so I put up with a certain amount of destruction by toddlers, and try to distract their attention rather than forbid them.

Small children love plants with unusual

descriptive names like bunnies' ears, lambs' lugs, lambs' tails and pussy willow, and evocative names like tiger lily and honeysuckle. You can teach your grandchildren to suck the nectar out of honeysuckle and montbretia flowers and to chew the juicy stems of grasses. You can show them how a snapdragon snaps, how foxglove flowers fit over your fingers and how to make a ballet dancer by turning back the petals of a poppy and binding its stem round the 'waist'.

Our summer ambition when we were children was to make the longest daisy chain in the world. It snaked across the lawn and back several times. On a more modest scale, you can start off with a necklace and bracelet, and a chain to go round a sunhat.

The Secret Garden

If you can persuade your grandchildren to let you read aloud to them Frances Hodgson Burnett's classic story, *The Secret Garden*, they will probably be hooked on gardens, if not on the hard graft of gardening, for life. The book describes the influence of a garden on a spoiled, mean-spirited, unloved child. By becoming involved with the seasonal cycle of renewal of life in the garden, Mary Lennox is herself transformed, learning to think about others and to make friends. Anyone who gets to the end of the story without shedding a tear is made of sterner stuff than me. The descriptions of the delight Mary and her new friends find in the miracle of growth in spring is somehow achieved without mawkish sentimentality: a miracle in itself when you consider that the author also wrote *Little Lord Fauntleroy*.

> '*It was the sweetest, most mysterious-looking place anyone could imagine… Everything was strange and silent, and she seemed to be hundreds of miles away from anyone, but somehow she did not feel lonely at all.*
>
> *The Secret Garden*, Frances Hodgson Burnett

Gardens can be of enormous significance for difficult children, like Mary Lennox or for children who are solitary by nature. If you have a grandchild with problems, allowing your garden to be their refuge, or spending time with them in the garden companionably, but with not much being said, may be the best way to establish a loving relationship with them.

… eight, nine, ten! Ready or not, I'm coming

Grandparents who live in the country are likely to be very popular with town-based families. One of the reasons grandchildren look forward to going to granny and grandpa's in the country is that they can offer the free-dom of a garden with space to run about and let off steam. The parents look forward to the visit too, because the children will not be on top of them all the time, and instead of having to take them to the park they can sit in deckchairs and read the papers.

For the grandparents, this is just as it should be. Probably because their own upbringing was based on fresh air and exercise as an essential part of their daily routine, it seems they love their grandchildren to be out-side as much as possible. Of the grannies I have talked to, most of them mentioned playing outside and hide-and-seek as favourite entertainments.

For many children, 'helping' granny and grandpa in the garden is just as fun as any game. Very little actual work gets done but a good time is had by all. The younger the helpers, the more willing they seem to be; as soon as they can walk they love an empty patch of earth to dig in, but when it comes to anything more complicated they are not as strong or as deft as their older siblings or cousins, and they are definitely weak on weed recogni-tion. They make up for what they lack in skill by display-ing great enthusiasm. For example, when you are prun-ing, if you hand the cuttings to a toddler one at a time, he will happily trot to and fro, carrying each twig to your wheelbarrow or basket. The reward is a ride in the wheelbarrow. 'I'll just get you a cushion, darling,' I said one time to my French-speaking grandson. A look of panic crossed his face. 'Not a pig, granny!' (as in *cochon*).

Toddlers will probably settle for child-sized garden tools, but as they grow older, these will soon be spurned in favour of the real thing. A five-year-old will do his best to wield a man-sized spade, and shift a full-sized wheelbarrow.

One job everyone can join in happily is raking and sweeping up the autumn leaves. Anyone not capable of raking or sweeping can use their hands to pile them up in the barrow or, which is more likely, take part in a leaf battle, throwing armfuls of leaves over each other. Once they have been transported to the bonfire and the bonfire has flared up and settled down to a smouldering glow, potatoes wrapped in foil can be put in to roast.

The flowers that bloom in the spring, tra-la

> *There are fairies at the bottom of our garden!*
> *It's not so very, very far away;*
> *You pass the gardener's shed and you just keep*
>   *straight ahead -*
> *I do so hope they've really come to stay.*
>   *Fairies*, by Rose Fyleman

I remember thinking when I was eight or nine that *The Flower Fairies Alphabet* was the most beautiful book I had ever seen. It was certainly a good way to learn the names of familiar flowers. Most gardens will have a fair selection of them growing in their beds and borders. The Columbine, Fuchsia, Lily of the Valley and Thrift fairies were my favourites.

A week seems like forever to a five-year-old, so when you and your grandchild are growing flowers from seed, choose those which give speedy results: among the quickest to germinate are bedding plants like Ageratum (5 to 14 days); Cosmos, Nicotiana and Petunia (7 to 14 days); French Marigold (2 to 7 days). However, they all need a warm atmosphere, and, in order for them to have a full summer flowering season, must be sown in early spring. This means, ideally, sowing them in a greenhouse, a propagator heated to the required temperature (18 to 25° C in most cases), or indoors on a light windowsill. If you grow them indoors, move them out as soon as the weather warms up or they will become very leggy.

Hardy annuals are much easier, as they can be sown outdoors straight into the ground, or else in pots. They can either remain in the pots or be planted out when they are a good size.

From a March sowing, in a normal summer, Alyssum, Candytuft and Limnanthes douglasii (poached egg plant) should flower in about 14 weeks. At that rate, seeds sown at halfterm in the spring term would be flowering in time for a summer halfterm visit, and if by any chance they were a failure, granny would have a chance to cheat a bit with a dash to the garden centre. Other easy favourites like Cornflowers, Calendula (Pot Marigold), Nasturtiums and Love-in-a-Mist take a week or two longer.

Planting bulbs is a very satisfactory occupation with children. Bulbs are easy to handle and there is no danger they will blow away, as there is with seeds, which are sometimes hardly more substantial than dust. They can be planted in autumn, in the ground or in pots, and forgotten about until spring when their pale, blunt shoots appear.

> 'She thought she saw something sticking out of the black earth — some sharp little pale green points.... "Yes, they are tiny growing things and they might be crocuses or snowdrops or daffodils," she whispered. She bent very close to them and sniffed the fresh scent of the damp earth. She liked it very much.'
>
> The Secret Garden, Frances Hodgson Burnett

Mr McGregor's Garden

> '*Now, my dears,*' said old Mrs. Rabbit one morning,
> '*you may go into the fields or down the lane, but*
> *don't go into Mr. McGregor's garden: your Father*
> *had an accident there; he was put in a pie by Mrs.*
> *McGregor.*'
>
> *The Story of Peter Rabbit*, Beatrix Potter

In the days of 'Digging for Victory' during World War II, when every inch of garden space was given over to home-grown produce, my brothers, cousins and I used to enjoy raiding our grandfather's vegetable patch. It was forbidden territory, but irresistible, and we felt as daring as Peter Rabbit. We stole succulent pods of peas and squirmed under the strawberry net to cram our mouths with fruit, appearing for lunch or tea with tell-tale stains on faces and hands. Our grandparents turned an indulgent blind eye.

Young children are fascinated by the idea of growing, harvesting and eating their own food. In the garden or on the allotment they love to help with digging potatoes, pulling carrots and picking peas and beans, although their attention span is short and they cannot be trusted to select only the ripest produce. Even the smallest garden could accommodate a small plot, or a couple of tubs or boxes for each child to grow his own crop. Radishes give the quickest results, and lettuces are quick too.

If you grow courgettes, you can personalise one or two by carving the children's names or initials on a small one and watching the name gradually get bigger as the courgette grows into a giant marrow. Sunflowers are fun to grow; they develop so fast and to such a spectacular size. Eventually, the seeds can be harvested to add to cereals for breakfast, or to feed the birds.

To encourage a long-term interest in your garden, choose a plant with special significance for each child: a shrub that blooms on that child's birthday, perhaps, or one that echoes the name of the child. You can nearly always find a rose to suit, there are so many to choose from, for example various members of my own family are catered for by 'Sophie's Perpetual', 'Janet's Pride', 'Robert le Diable' and 'Master Hugh'.

Worthwhile investments

• *A sandpit.* Even in small gardens there is always room for a sandpit, which gives very good value in terms of hours of play in all seasons when the weather is reasonably mild. A sandpit must have a cover to prevent cats from using it as a lavatory and to stop bugs and leaves falling in. It need not be expensive.

Ours is a green plastic turtle which I am pretty sure has offended the aesthetic sensibilities of a number of visitors to the garden. 'Never explain, never apologise,' I remind myself.

If I were starting again I would make a sandpit out of more sympathetic materials: larch poles or railway sleepers for the sides, on a waterproof base of plastic sheeting. The sides should be high enough and chunky enough for children to sit on – you, too, ideally. The lid can be a simple arrangement of plastic sheeting nailed to a timber frame, or you could just spread the sheet over and anchor it with large stones or bricks. A more ambitious and ornamental structure could be made on the understanding that, when the children grow out of playing with sand, it can be converted into a small pond. The best kind of sand is silver sand, obtainable from garden centres and Mothercare.

With a few small buckets and spades, or just plastic bowls, yoghurt pots and kitchen spoons, it will seem almost as good as being on the beach. When the sand becomes smelly or begins to green up with algae, it can be sterilised by watering on a solution of the liquid used to sterilise babies' bottles. 'No throwing sand' has to be a strictly enforced rule.

• *A swing.* We have an old ash tree with a stout horizontal branch just begging to have a swing slung from it, a proper, traditional swing, with a wooden seat hung from ropes. The trouble with a swing is, that until children are old enough to swing themselves without a push, a grown-up has to be in attendance. I use it quite a lot myself when I am sure no-one is looking.

• *A truck.* I can recommend a four-wheeled trolley called 'Radio Flyer'. After four years rough usage, it seems to be indestructible. It is much in demand as a train taking small passengers from one 'station' to another. You will have to be the engine pulling it unless there are good-natured older children to pull the little ones. The older children have fun with it, hurtling down a steep bank and falling off at the bottom. It also does garden duty, transporting rubbish to the compost heap or bonfire.

• *Climbing frame and slide.* This is so expensive that it is probably only worth investing in if you have a lot of grandchildren who visit you often, and if you don't live in walking distance of a park with a playground.

• *Trampoline.* Even more hideously expensive, but all grandparents who have bought one say that their grandchildren have become completely addicted and are happily occupied all day long. Perhaps worth investing if you are going to use it yourself.

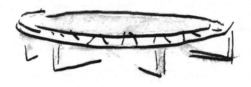

Bats and balls

A MUM SAYS:
She spends hours bowling cricket balls.

GRANDCHILDREN SAY:
Granny is a jolly good bowler, considering.

Children under five love just kicking a ball, or trying to hit it with a racket or bat. They don't have to score a goal or hit the ball over the net. Just throwing the ball from a few feet away for them to catch or hit is good practice, to develop hand-eye co-ordination, even if they only manage to catch it once in ten times. Throwing endless dropped catches is just the sort of patient, mind-numbing task at which Good Grannies excel.

When very small children are involved it is much easier not to have winners or losers, unless you can somehow guarantee that everyone wins (the Caucus race again). It is very difficult to organise a fair competition. The little ones pick the football up and run with it, or score own goals, and the older ones get exasperated. The important thing is to ensure that everyone gets a turn.

I am reluctant to mention Croquet. It can be played on any vaguely rectangular lawn that is reasonably level. The reason for my reluctance is that it is the most annoying game ever invented: character forming, perhaps, but absolutely infuriating.

If you are a keen gardener, you will want to make a few basic rules to protect your garden. But don't aim for perfection: an occasional ball is sure to be kicked into a flowerbed and a branch will be snapped off by a tree-climber now and then.

Tents, tepees and Wendy houses

Of course the Neverlands vary a good deal... John lived in a boat turned upside down on the sands, Michael in a wigwam, Wendy in a house of leaves deftly sewn together.

Peter Pan, J.M. Barrie

Children seem to have an instinctive wish for a den or shelter of their own. Crawlers as well as toddlers enjoy having a semi-private snug space to hide in, too. A play-sized tent is as good indoors as out, but an improvised arrangement of a blanket or bedspread draped over the table, big enough to come down to the ground, does just as well.

Ready-made playhouses, or Wendy houses, are immensely popular, providing, as they do, scope for all sorts of role-playing games. But they are also immensely expensive, and, if your budget does not run to one, a very large cardboard box, the kind a washing machine might be delivered in, does duty as a house. Let them use their initiative to furnish it; offer only the gentlest of hints how they might go about it.

Little ones enjoy games involving a frisson of fear. Grandpa playing the part of the big bad wolf, huffing and puffing till he blows their house in sends our grandchildren into delighted hysteria, though the more timid among them do show signs of anxiety when he goes into his Jack Nicholson 'Here's Johnnie' routine.

Making your own shelter taps into a primitive urge and is deeply satisfying. With minimal help from grown-ups, five or six-year-olds can make a willow or bamboo

Bamboo or willow wigwam/tepee

1. Push 4,6 or 8 bamboo canes or willow shoots into the ground to form a square, hexagon or octagon.

2. Gather the canes or shoots together at the top and tie them firmly.

3. Drape an old sheet, table cloth or bedspread over the structure and fasten it to the framework with garden wire.

4. Get the children to paint totemic emblems on the material.

hide or a tepee improvised with bean-poles and a blanket. Willow structures have the advantage of continuing to grow, producing leafy shoots that can be woven into the original structure for extra cover and stability. There is an old wives' tale that says willow rods are best harvested under a waning moon and planted under a waxing moon – just the sort of information that a Good Granny hands down to her grandchildren. This is the kind of project that grandparents must not hijack; it is tempting, when you see children making a bit of a mess of a job, to take over and do it properly yourself – thereby spoiling their fun. Your role should simply be to get them off to a good start, and give help only when called upon to do so.

From school age onwards, your grandchildren will want to find their own secret place to make a den, without your knowledge. It will probably be the most neglected part of the garden, hidden among dense shrubs. It may even be up a tree; in my grandparents' garden there was an ancient mulberry with low branches, which could accommodate a secret society consisting of half a dozen cousins. You need to be aware of any secret hidey-hole, so you know the children are safe, but don't let on that you know their secret.

The birds and the bees

I saw a little bird go hop, hop, hop,
And I said 'Little bird, won't you stop, stop stop?'
I ran to the window to say 'How do you do?'
But he shook his little tail and away he flew.

Children love feeding the birds. When they come on a winter visit, putting out seed on the bird table is an enjoyable daily ritual, and watching the birds gives the children a chance to learn how to identify the different species. Most pet shops and garden shops sell suitable seed mixes for wild birds. If you have a bird table you have probably positioned it high up, out of the reach of cats and squirrels. It will also be out the reach of children, so, rather than have to lift each child up to it, when they are with you, put a tray of seed and water on a low table, which the children can reach easily to replenish it.

They can make a peanut necklace to hang up for the tits and other small birds. Buy peanuts in their shells and, using a large needle and strong cotton, thread them through the centre of each shell.

A swarm of bees in May
Is worth a load of hay.
A swarm of bees in June

Is worth a silver spoon.
A swarm of bees in July
Isn't worth a fly.

If you keep bees, you can tell your older grandchildren about the old superstition of 'telling the bees'. You are supposed to go to your hives and tell the bees any family news such as births, marriages and deaths, otherwise they will forsake the hive.

Pond life

The water was all slippy sloppy in the larder and in
the back passage. But Mr Jeremy liked getting his feet
wet; nobody scolded him and he never caught a cold!
The Tale of Mr Jeremy Fisher, Beatrix Potter

Among my happiest childhood memories are visits to 'the dibble-dabble'. The dibble-dabble was a series of narrow ponds linked by little waterfalls, in the garden of Mr Shaw Mellor, about whom my grandmother used to make up rhymes.

My grandmother used to leave us to play in this little paradise while she discussed parish business with her friend. There was also a fountain in his garden on which you could, if you were clever, balance a ping-pong ball.

The ponds were full of sticklebacks and frogspawn, and empty jam jars were supplied for us to catch them in to take home.

If you want to start a small wildlife pond for your grandchildren's benefit or your own, all you need is a suitable receptacle (half an oak barrel will do nicely, or a plastic baby's bath) and half a gallon of water from an established pond as a 'starter'. Add this primeval soup to the water in your pond and it will soon be teeming with life. For an indoor pond you simply leave the starter water in a gallon bottle with air holes in the lid.

Watering the garden and washing the car.

As I touched on earlier, your grandchildren will enjoy helping you wash the car enormously, although they will probably be more of a hindrance than a help. If you keep a tricycle or toy car or tractor at your house, they will be just as happy washing that, while you wash the car, and will have the satisfaction of completing the job unaided.

Watering the garden is another popular occupation,

either with a watering can of manageable size or with a hose. The water will go everywhere except where you want it to. These water-based jobs are really only for a warm summer day, as, no matter what precautions you take, your grandchild will end up soaking wet and so, probably, will you. On a really hot day, nothing is so much fun for little children as stripping off and scampering to and fro under a lawn sprinkler.

PART III **THE BIG ISSUES**

This section deals with aspects of childcare that are notoriously difficult for parents and, by implication, for grandparents too. You will probably remember the battles you had with your own children about food, bedtime and discipline. The good news is that grandparents don't have to tackle these issues head on. But it does help to be aware of what your grandchildren's parents are trying to achieve, and to recognise the pitfalls so that you can tiptoe around them.

CHAPTER 9   FOOD

To granny's house I go,
That I may fatter grow
                    The Story of Lambkin. Anon

It always astonished me that I could make my grand-
mother go into raptures of joy just by being hungry.
The Words, Jean Paul Sartre

The food of love

One of the ways we show love for our children and grandchildren is by feeding them. This basic instinct, to do with the survival of the species, has become refined into the deep satisfaction we get from cooking their favourite dishes, and giving them special treats. Happy memories about grandparents are often to do with food. When we went to Sunday lunch with my grandparents, more often than not the pudding was Walls vanilla ice-cream served with a delicious fudgy gunge which granny made by boiling a tin of condensed milk for about four hours.

One friend recalls a tram ride with granny to meet grandpa at the end of his working day, and a three-pence bag of chips as a treat on the way home. Did the food always taste better because it was served with love?

GRANDCHILDREN SAY:
Granny's cucumber sandwiches with the crusts cut off represented time, care and love. And bread slices as thin as lace and butter just right.

Nan was a big, big lady but always very cuddly and welcoming and always made us special drinks, ice-creams, etc.

I will forever associate Weetabix with my grandmother. Weetabix with caster sugar (which we never had at home) on the yellow Formica table in her kitchen.

My best friend at junior school used to take me to her grandma's because, she said, 'She'll offer us a sherry.' And she did without fail.

Much of our generation's nostalgia for our grandparents' food is focused on 'afternoon tea', a meal that is all but extinct today. My grandfather would routinely say at teatime, as my grandmother heaped homemade strawberry jam on to my bread-and-butter: 'In my young days we were allowed butter or jam, never both.' Other grannies of today remember their grandparents making 'dainty sandwiches and pretty cakes', and 'legendary rum babas'.

The affection generated by a grandmother's loving care expressed through food is sometimes even transferred to the utensils she used. According to the historian Suetonius, in *Lives of the Twelve Caesars*, the Emperor Vespasian was accustomed, on all special occasions, to drink out of a silver cup habitually used by his grandmother Tertulla, who brought him up. Leaping forward to the 21st century, a mother tells how she still uses her grandmother's cooking equipment: 'I recently broke the dish she used every Christmas for raspberry jelly, and it felt like breaking a close link with her.'

Breast or bottle

Food can become a point of contention even before the baby is born, when the parents-to-be are deciding whether the baby will be breastfed or bottle-fed. Many grannies bottle-fed their own babies, and don't see the point of breastfeeding. If you are one of those, it may be best to keep your opinion to yourself.

Nowadays breastfeeding is much more common, as you will see if you encounter young mums and their babies on the bus, in the park, in museums and art galleries, in fact in virtually any public place.

Today's parents don't find it at all embarrassing, and have breastfed their babies in, among other places, the shoe department of John Lewis, the lobby at Claridges Hotel and in church. However, breastfeeding is not yet allowed in the House of Commons.

Expectant parents have probably read all the books and been thoroughly briefed by their midwife, so if all you can think of to say in favour of the bottle is 'Well, it never did you any harm', you would do well to swallow your pride and ask to borrow the books, so you can understand the up-to-date theory. Better still, health authorities in some parts of the country organise ante-natal classes specifically designed for grandparents. Grandfathers as well as grandmothers are welcomed, and nobody mocks you for believing old granny tales like the one that says you shouldn't eat peas while you are breast-feeding. Or the one about lemon upsetting the baby. They will just ease you gently into the paths of modern baby-care righteousness.

MUMS SAY:

My mum didn't breastfeed, bitterly regretted it and encouraged me to breastfeed. Both of my parents have been so supportive over this, I am amazed and glad-dened. My dad always finds me a chair which will be comfortable to feed in....

My mother-in-law was initially very uncomfortable and sceptical about me breastfeeding, because she had had problems with it, but once I had explained I real-ly wanted to give it my best shot and then she saw her grandson getting bigger by the minute, she changed her mind and now she boasts about her breastfeeding daughter-in-law and her fat and happy grandchildren.

New mothers are easily rattled, especially when the child they are feeding is their first. One mum told me she found it quite devastating when her own mother urged her to give up breastfeeding. She realised that her mother was worried about her because she was having difficulties and was terribly tired all the time, but she longed for her mother to support her in her determination to keep trying.

In the early weeks of a baby's life, Good Grannies take a back seat. Controversy may rage about breast versus bottle, and demand feeding versus strict routine. But your nurturing instinct will be best satisfied by feeding the new baby's parents and siblings, if any.

Fussy eaters

What is the matter with Mary Jane?
She's perfectly well and she hasn't a pain
And it's lovely rice pudding for dinner again.
What is the matter with Mary Jane?
      Rice Pudding, A.A. Milne

Food is a marvellously potent form of blackmail, and parents all too often allow meals to become an exhausting battleground where the result is at best a draw. Children are quick to learn that rejecting the food on offer is the easiest way to manipulate the adults around them.

Persistent rejection of pasta because it is 'the wrong shape' and other foods because they are too hot, too cold, too wet, too crunchy, too oily or simply not pink enough, can cause mothers to lose their temper or burst into tears. One mum admits to having poured a bowl of cereal and milk over her two-year-old's head, another to 'abjectly following my daughter round the room with a banana trying to coax her to have little nibbles'.

In a survey of 2000 grandmothers carried out by *Yours* magazine in 2004, 37% of the grannies thought their grandchildren were 'fussy eaters'. Most of the grannies I have talked to would agree, and feel it is a mistake to encourage a fussy attitude by offering toddlers a choice of food or drink.

GRANNIES SAY:
The parents give them too much choice: they behave like waiters and waitresses.

The children are never made to finish, and also they ask for different things.

My daughter panders to them and their whims – mad.

Too many choices, too big helpings.

She cooks several different meals for each child – something I would never have done.

MUMS SAY:
My mother assumed I could make Victoria eat what was put in front of her, but it was impossible.

When we visit the grandparents, they sometimes find it difficult adjusting mealtimes around the children.

She doesn't approve of them being brought up vegetarian and I've had constant criticism for that.

Asking children to choose puts a burden on them. They may be happier, for example, just to be given either apple juice or orange juice rather than have to decide which they want. If you think the parents are getting things wrong, when you are in charge you can discreetly redress the balance. It is all right to have different rules at your house about, for example, sitting down together to eat (something almost all grannies agree is important) and finishing what is on your plate, provided it is a token, very small helping. But you should stick to the parents' rules about what the children are allowed to eat and what is frowned upon for health or other reasons.

Most of the grannies I consulted were adamant that children should 'try everything and have a very small helping of less favourite things', or 'be made to taste just a little of everything.' One granny's sensible advice was, 'Only put a small amount on the plate, so a clean plate can be achieved easily – and more is then often asked for.'

Some grannies are more successful than others. One daughter-in-law said, full of awe, 'She got all the children to eat *everything*.' I wish I knew her secret. On the few occasions I have tried it, the conversation went something like this:

> 'What's that, granny?'
> 'Kedgeree, darling. It's absolutely delicious.'
> 'I don't like it.'
> 'You don't know till you try it. Just have a little taste.'
> 'No. I don't like it.'
> 'You don't know till you try it…'
> 'I don't *like* it, granny.'

What do you say next? 'Just eat three tiny mouthfuls and you can have ice-cream for pudding?' I don't think so. Bribery leads to blackmail. Naturally you will try all your winning ways and powers of persuasion to get the children to eat up, but be warned that, once you start with eating 'games' you may be stuck with them at every meal. So think twice before you pretend the spoonful of spinach is an aeroplane, or offer one for Mummy, one for Daddy, one for the dog, one for the gerbil and so on.

Having said that, a game of 'Restaurants' has become a favourite with my own grandchildren – once they are past the highchair stage. They start by writing a menu, with a little prompting from me, based on what I know is in the fridge. Then, when lunch or supper time arrives, they are customers in a restaurant and I am the waiter:

> *Me*: Good evening, sir. Are you ready to order?
> *Max (looking at the menu)*: Yes, I'll have pancakes and jam and ice-cream.
> *Me*: I'm sorry, sir, but we're out of pancakes. May I recommend the fish fingers? They are fresh in this morning. And would sir care for some broccoli, and some ketchup?
> *Max*: Thank you, waiter. And please bring me some juice.

It seems to make meals pass with fewer arguments, and just occasionally the children are so wrapped up in the game that they inadvertently eat something they are normally convinced they don't like. Fortunately, one of the joys of grandparenthood as opposed to parenthood is that you can take the easy way out with a clear conscience. The easy way out at mealtimes is to give them what they like. Good Grannies' advice includes 'Respect their dislikes' and 'If they make a fuss, take the food away'.

If I remember right, food was not such a big problem when our children were small. I don't like to own up to this, but mine were fed almost exclusively on fish fingers, beef burgers, spaghetti hoops, Findus crispy pancakes, chips and frozen peas. Afters were either Birds Angel Delight, Chocolate Lovelies or mousses that came in little jelly-mould shaped plastic pots (their name escapes me). This limited diet did not affect the children's health and, in the long term, did not affect their attitude to food. They have both, in their different ways, turned out to be gourmets. It may reassure parents to remind them that they, too, were 'fussy eaters' once.

When I was a young mother, I had never heard the word 'organic' and very little dietary advice came my way. Surely it was the same for most mums in the 1960s? I suppose we were aware that sugar rotted the teeth, but for all we knew, 'Salmonella' might have been the sister of the TV cartoon character Aqua Marina, beloved of 'Marine Boy'. Mercifully, Mad Cow Disease was also as yet undiscovered.

Today, quite rightly, many parents insist on organic meat and vegetables and free range eggs and poultry at home, and they expect grandparents to serve up the same. They may also have other rules. It is now well established that salt is dangerous for babies under one, and in many families sugar is frowned on, especially in the form of sweets and ice-cream.

If they are forbidden, do granny and grandpa get a special dispensation to break the rules? They need not be afraid of setting a harmful precedent. From an early age children can distinguish between everyday and special occasions – they will accept without rancour that mum's reply to 'Granny always lets me …' is likely to be an emphatic 'Well I don't'.

Staying within the permitted parameters, in theory the cuisine at granny's and grandpa's can be as varied as they care to make it. In practice, it will be restricted by what the children are prepared to eat. You will want your grandchildren to have a wonderful time when they visit you, so, before they come, check their likes and dislikes, and

Menu off fuood
fish fingers
Pancakes
Pasta
Chips
bread
jam
Marmite
ketchup
ham
avo
tuna fish
broccli
ice cream

make sure your information is up to date. If you bought honey loops because your grandchild liked them last time, and it turns out he will now only eat rice krispies, day one will get off to a bad start. It can be complicated, so, if in doubt, get it in writing. Here is a list kindly drawn up by the parents of Max, aged $4^1/_2$, and Guy, $1^1/_2$, for grandparents left in charge for a few days:

Food Guide

Breakfast:

Max will only eat either Cheerios (called honey loops) without milk, toast and marmite or bread and marmite, plus drink of cranberry juice 50/50 with water in cup with a lid with one teaspoon fish oil added (in fridge).

Guy will have either Cheerios, Shreddies or Rice Krispies with milk, plus toast sometimes.

Main courses:

Fish fingers
Pizza
Plain pasta with tomato sauce and cheese
Stuffed spinach and ricotta pasta with butter and cheese
Fish cakes

Chicken breast cut into pieces and stir fried with garlic butter and squeeze of lemon juice
Ham (must remove all traces of fat for Max)
Chicken goujons (not nuggets, unless home-made)
Tuna
Tinned sardines (good mixed with rice or pasta)
Sausages – chipolatas from the butcher
Guy also likes eggs (scrambled or boiled) but Max won't touch them

Vegetables & Fruit:
Carrots
Broccoli
Cauliflower
Avocado
Guy also likes peas and sweetcorn
Mashed potato, chips, baked potato (Max likes you to take it out of the skin and turn it into mashed potato)
Max loves apples and grapes, Guy may deign to eat a ripe pear

Yoghurt:
Max likes 'pink' best, won't touch banana flavour
Guy not fussy but has annoying habit of taking lid off, smearing it all over table, and not eating it

Perhaps things haven't changed so much since the 1960s after all. Above all, the key to happy mealtimes is to be relaxed. It is inevitably worrying, even more for parents than for grandparents, when a child will eat practically nothing, but in most cases the child will thrive in spite of a restricted diet. One granny, rather surprised and relieved, reported, 'My daughter does not insist on her son eating his food – and he seems to survive on very little and to be taller and even stronger than his cousin.' Children who are fussy eaters at home sometimes gobble up their school dinners, and are happy to eat what is put in front of them in their friends' houses.

Table manners

> *I eat my peas with honey*
> *I've done so all my life.*
> *It may seem rather funny*
> *But it keeps them on the knife*
> Anon

Grandparents' own perception is that they set more store by good table manners, indeed, good manners in general, than parents do. Perhaps it is because they do not have the daily task of trying to instil them.

They agree that manners do not come naturally; they

have to be taught, and before they can be taught, the child has to master a few basic skills. For a baby trying to feed herself, learning the necessary skills is bound to involve a certain amount of mess, and this is where one of the Good Granny's most useful attributes, patience, comes into play.

Babies vary a lot in the time it takes them to learn to eat tidily, using a spoon. Most of them enjoy the challenge of picking up small bits of food, such as individual peas, etc. They also enjoy throwing food on the floor whilst eyeing you in a challenging way. If you have a dog, he will position himself in easy reach of the high chair and hoover up the scraps. If not, a mat or plastic sheet under the high chair can make tidying up easier. Equip yourself with a non-spill mug if that is what the baby is used to, and have a roll of kitchen paper handy for wiping the table, the floor, the dog, yourself and the baby.

Once your grandchild can more or less feed himself, there is really no excuse for bad table manners. Grannies seem to care about this a good deal:

GRANNIES SAY:
My grandchildren have appalling table manners when they're at home. I cannot stand them. When I have them on their own they behave impeccably.

I tend to come down too hard on them.

Table manners need to be taught.

With me, they have to stay sitting at the table.

I've given up on this.

One wise granny pointed out that the better man-nered they are the easier they will find being in company later on in life. In our own household, when we have our grandchildren on their own, we follow their parents' lead, constantly remind them about 'please' and 'thank you', about offering food to others before helping your-self, and asking to 'get down' or 'leave the table' at the end of a meal. The hope is that endless, monotonous rep-etition will hammer the message home.

We try to remember not to correct the children's manners in *front* of their parents. My father-in-law once ticked our son off for his bad table manners. Hugh was picking the icing off a cake and his grandpa leaned over, rapped his knuckles with the back of a spoon and said sharply: 'Don't piggle'. Hugh was very surprised and so was I. I was also infuriated at the implied criticism of my methods of upbringing. It happened more than thirty years ago, but I still remember it vividly.

Granny's little helper

Half a pound of tuppenny rice,
Half a pound of treacle,
That's the way the money goes,
Pop goes the weasel.

Children love cooking. This means you can do things you were going to do anyway in the kitchen, with your grand-children as bystanders and participants. You just have to accept that, when children help, everything is liable to take twice as long, and plan accordingly. It speeds things up if you give them a special job, then quietly get on with what you have to do, involving them at key moments and allowing them to taste at different stages. Tasting is an important part of learning how to be a good cook. Thinking about whether a cake mix needs more sugar, or is chocolatey enough, may have a beneficial side-effect by making the children more interested in tasting new food at other times.

Cooking with children raises safety issues. Throughout the book I have assumed that you will keep your grand-children safe by applying common sense, and have only mentioned a few precautions that their parents tend to nag us about. But it seems sensible to remind you that it is never too young to learn that 'hot' means dangerous, knives are sharp and you should never ever put your fingers near an electric whisk or food mixer.

Children of five or younger can, with a little practice and careful supervision safely handle a potato peeler. They can help weigh out ingredients, they can break eggs (but not separate yolks from whites) and they can stir mixtures. They love peeling hard-boiled eggs, but probably won't want to eat them. Very carefully supervised, they can cut up fruit and grate cheese.

> *The Queen of hearts, she made some tarts,*
> *All on a summer's day.*

Biscuits, pies and tarts are especially satisfying to make because they are so tactile. Pastry dough, bought or home-made, will withstand any amount of roly-poly and squeezing in pudgy little hands, although the end product may not melt in the mouth after so much handling. A recipe for a robust and foolproof biscuit dough is given below. If you make bread, kneading the dough and dividing it to make rolls is a very satisfactory occupation for children.

You need an apron for each child; if you have to improvise, tie a tea towel round the child's neck and roll up her sleeves. It is worth investing in one or more (one for each child, to avoid arguments) pastry boards, unless the surface of your kitchen table or worktop is suitable, and a rolling pin for each child. Child-sized rolling pins, available from kitchenware shops or toyshops, are easiest for small hands to use. A flour-sifter is useful. Tape the lid on with masking tape or Sellotape to stop it falling off when shaken. Pastry cutters can be bought in all sorts of shapes, such as moon and stars, gingerbread men and farm animals, and plain round cutters are useful to make individual tarts or biscuits to decorate as faces. If you can make washing-up afterwards form part of the project, so much the better.

Biscuit dough

100g / 4oz butter
100g / 4oz sugar
175g / 6oz plain flour
1 egg

Whizz all ingredients together in the food processor. Roll out on a floured board or worktop, cut into shapes.

Cook at 180ºC, 350ºF, Gas mark 4 for 10-15 minutes. When cool, ice and decorate.

When we were children cake-making was a satisfying and lengthy ritual involving a lot of elbow grease, creaming butter and sugar. Nowadays it is a matter of throwing all the ingredients into the food processor and giving it a whizz. Nostalgia is not a good reason for making things more complicated than they need be, and today's children are happy just to weigh out the butter, flour and sugar, break the eggs and switch the machine on. There is still a bowl to lick and that was always the best part. Whether you make a big cake or individual little cakes in paper cases, icing and decorating is fun: you can sieve icing sugar or icing sugar mixed with cocoa over the top, or spread glacé icing or butter icing, coloured as luridly as the cooks like, then sprinkle on hundreds and thousands or press Smarties in.

Jelly on a plate, jelly on a plate
Wibble-wobble, wibble-wobble, jelly on a plate.

Jelly never goes out of style. If you need the excuse of a party to make it and serve it, give a party for the dolls and teddies. Jelly moulds come in all shapes and sizes, but if you have none, it is easy to improvise with glasses, cups and ramekins. Small fruits like raspberries and redcurrants can be suspended in jelly, as can edible flowers like primroses, marigolds and nasturtiums. Home-made jelly made from fruit juice is a good way to con children who won't eat fruit into consuming it, and jelly made with flavoured milk goes down a treat with non-milk-drinkers.

It is, perhaps, a pity that we invariably make sweet foods when we cook with children. There is no reason why the pastry should not be made into cheese straws, and experiments undertaken by mashing up tinned tuna and adding crème fraiche or mayonnaise until it tastes right. Children also enjoy making pizza. Scone dough makes a good base, and they love 'dressing' it with tomato purée, grated cheese, chopped ham and anything else that happens to be lurking in the fridge.

Sweets and treats

> I know a little cupboard,
> With a teeny tiny key,
> And there's a jar of Lollypops
> For me, me, me.
>
> It has a little shelf, my dear,
> As dark as dark can be,
> And there's a dish of Banbury Cakes
> For me, me, me.
>
> I have a small fat grandmamma,
> With a very slippery knee,

And she's Keeper of the Cupboard
With the key, key, key.

And when I'm very good, my dear,
As good as good can be,
There's Banbury Cakes and Lollypops
For me, me, me.

The Cupboard, Walter de la Mare, 1904

A GRANNY SAYS:
My only memory of my paternal grandmother is that she kept currants in a tall cupboard in the kitchen and would give me a handful as a treat.

There was always a sweetie jar in grandma's house.

Today's grandparents remember sweets with nostalgia as part of their relationship with their own grandparents. My own granny always brought out a tin of McIntosh's Quality Street after lunch. There was a picture of a lady in a pink crinoline on the lid. We were only allowed one chocolate each, and I delved for the one in the violet cellophane wrapper, which I liked best (still do).

At the end of lunch with my other grandmother, Ginny, we used to cluster round her chair, waiting, like baby birds with open beaks, for our 'canard' – a sugar lump which she would dip into her cup of coffee, and then drop into each child's mouth.

The giving of sweets, ice-creams, crisps and other junk food treats can be an issue between parents and grandparents. Parents today are more conscious than we were of the damage that sugary and fatty foods can do if they arc a regular part of a child's diet, and many parents have strict rules about their consumption. Some modern parents do use sweets and biscuits shamelessly as bribes (or as 'rewards', in which case less shame attaches). A granny told me that her three-year-old grandson had to have two rotting teeth extracted: not her fault but the parents'. But most parents limit sweets as strictly as my grandparents did. And they expect grandparents to observe their rules.

MUMS COMPLAIN:
This was the source of the biggest row; I said NO sweets so my parents and in-laws fell over themselves to feed Smarties the moment my back was turned.

They hand out far too many sweets, HUGE Easter eggs, etc.

GRANNIES SAY:
I'm not allowed to give sweets, chocolate or ice-cream – nearly all treats are in the gift of the parents! But I do long to buy chocolate Teddy-bears.

What's grandparenting if you can't spoil them?

MUMS SAY:
My mother-in-law is a wonderful granny. She never has sweets or biscuits in her house and only gives her grandkids good wholesome food and snacks.

I am delighted that my parents do all the things that we, as parents, can't or won't, e.g. take them AT LAST to Macdonalds.

If your grandchildren's parents do have rules, and you do break them, don't suppose for a moment that you won't be found out. The children may not squeal on you, but someone else will. There is an ice-cream van which parks just round the corner from my grandson Max's primary school (it shouldn't be allowed). I was taken unawares the first time I collected him from school, and fell for his entreaties to buy him and his younger brother Guy each a cornet with a chocolate flake stuck in it (anything for a quiet life). We have to cross a railway bridge to get home, so I made them stand still and eat their ice-creams, fearing a scene if the ice-cream should drop out of the cornet onto the railway below. As we stood there, several mothers and children on their way home grinned and said hello. The next few days, I brought bread to feed the ducks and took the long route home, by the river, so as to avoid the ice cream van. Then my daughter and son-in-law returned from their holiday and I went home. The next time I saw them, after we had exchanged our news, my daughter said, 'I hear you bought them an ice-cream on the way home from school.' She was amused rather than annoyed, but I still felt like a naughty schoolgirl.

Perhaps for nostalgic reasons of their own, parents are often much more indulgent about the giving of sweet treats if the said treats are home-made – and particularly if they know the children have had the fun of helping to make them themselves. My own children went through a sweet-making phase when they were little, and much enjoyed it. They started with peppermint creams which needed no cooking, and graduated to fudge.

Eating out

One of the changes since we were children and since our children were little, is the way children eat out with their

Hugh's Peppermint Creams

460g / 1lb icing sugar
1 egg white
$^1/_2$ cup double cream
Peppermint essence

Sieve the icing sugar. Add the rest of the ingredients and stir until smooth.

Dust a board or worktop with icing sugar, roll out the paste and use a cutter to stamp into rounds.

Put on a wire rack to dry for 12 hours.

parents on a regular basis. I may have led an exceptionally sheltered life, but I don't think I saw the inside of a café or restaurant until my tenth birthday, when my grandmother Ginny took us to Gunter's, an immensely elegant tea shop in Park Lane. This was her regular birthday treat for all her grandchildren, sometimes at Gunter's and sometimes (oh joy!) the soda fountain at Fortnum and Mason. Our own children were aged at least seven and six by the time we started meeting up with friends and their children for a curry at Sunday lunchtimes.

Nowadays, nobody wants to be left at home minding the baby (although this is a role the Good Granny can usefully perform occasionally), so they take the baby along too. This was brought home to me one afternoon, when Max was about $3^{1}/_{2}$, and he and I were on our way home from the park. 'Shall we go to the pub, Granny Jane?' he asked as we approached The Bell and Crown with its outdoor, riverside tables. I remembered then that the first time Max went to a restaurant was at the age of three months when we all went out to dinner. On that occasion he was fretful and we had to take turns pushing the pram up and down the pavement outside. That is something the Good Granny is prepared to volunteer for, but it may not be necessary. On other occasions each of our grandchildren, when they were still infants, have slept happily through lunches and dinners out.

Another grandson, Oscar, is half French and knows almost instinctively where the best hot chocolate and *pain au chocolat* are served. The first time he stayed at school all day, including school dinner, he came home with shining eyes to announce 'They have a *Restaurant* at school.'

If you are out and about with small children, they and you need fuelling at frequent intervals. The only time I have had problems has been at lunchtime when visiting museums or other attractions. I assumed that we could easily get lunch at the museum restaurant or cafeteria, but the queues for a table, or for self-service were so horrendous I gave up in despair. With a little forward planning I could have brought a simple picnic and followed it up with an ice-cream, or, better still, booked a table at a modest Italian restaurant a street away. Children enjoy sitting down and being waited on, and choosing from a menu. It makes them feel grown-up. If I am with toddlers I avoid self-serve places like the plague – how can you hold on to a roaming child and steer your cafeteria tray along the counter at the same time? Child-friendly chains like Pizza Express and Giraffe are a much easier option, especially for children who are still at the high chair stage.

For older children, a restaurant meal à deux (à trois if grandpa comes too) can be very special for the grandparents as well as the child.

CHAPTER 10 – BEDTIME

Rub-a-dub-dub, three men in a tub,
The butcher, the baker, the candlestick maker,
They all jumped out on a rotten potato.

Hush-a-bye, baby, on the tree top,
When the wind blows the cradle will rock.
When the bough breaks the cradle will fall
Down will come baby, cradle and all.

The end of the day can be the best part, and bathtime and story time the greatest fun. But it doesn't always work out like that because your grandchildren's parents are shattered with fatigue, the children are tired and grouchy and you find yourself being short-tempered and snappy and hurrying things along. When this happens, just keep in your mind's eye an image of a cup of tea, gin-

and-tonic, glass of chilled Sauvignon blanc, or whatever it is you will indulge in once they are safely tucked up.

Bathtime

For tiny babies bathtime need not always come at the end of the day. It can be at any time, and, if the baby is not tired or hungry, the bath is one of life's great pleasures, not just for the parents and grandparents but for the child too. He is literally in his element, enjoying the sensation of being surrounded by water just as he was in his mother's womb and kicks and stretches and gurgles with pleasure. If the baby's mother or father forgets to offer you a ringside seat, ask nicely for one. Your request is not likely to be refused unless, as has been known to happen from time to time, your son-in-law is actually getting in the bath with the baby.

After a few times as a spectator, you may be allowed to bath the baby yourself. Some things have changed since the days when bathing babies was second nature to you. The bath is not always a daily ritual. Twice or even once a week is considered enough provided careful topping and tailing is carried out every day. Soap is frowned upon for babies with sensitive skin, and people no longer poke cotton wool buds into crevices and orifices. Talcum powder is now taboo, as the baby may breathe in tiny particles, which can irritate the lungs. But mothers and fathers still test the water temperature with an elbow, babies still squirm and wriggle, and boys will still squirt you in the eye as soon as you have them naked on your lap. You don't need me to tell you that you must never ever leave a child alone in the bath even for a few seconds. If the phone rings, just don't answer.

Most toddlers and young children love bathtime, and the problem is getting them out of the bath rather than getting them into it. If you have a reluctant bather, give a bright and breezy early warning 'bathtime in five minutes' then get the bath ready before you bring your powers of persuasion to bear. Your grandchild probably objects more to having his play interrupted than to the bath itself, so assemble a good selection of bath toys, so he can look forward to granny's boat or octopus or rubber duck.

When my grandchildren are reluctant to go upstairs at bathtime they usually let me jump them up, 'like a kangaroo'. The child goes in front and you support him by holding his hands from behind while his legs clamber up two steps at a time.

Undressing can be a game, too, with variations on peek-a-boo' and 'skin a rabbit'. One is supposed to encourage children to undress themselves as soon as they are capable of doing so, but it takes more than twice as long.

One of my grandsons likes to prance naked around the house at this stage, teasing me, or his parents, by refusing to get into the bath. Joining in the game and trying to catch him has turned out to be a big mistake, so now I ignore him and kneel by the bath, playing with the bath toys myself. If you have no toys, yoghurt pots and a squirty washing-up liquid bottle are nearly as good. Just pouring water from a height from one container into another usually makes him want to join in. Once you have the child in the bath, let him wash himself if that is what he

likes to do – it doesn't matter if neither he nor you do a very thorough job – and don't attempt a hair wash unless you are in charge for more than a few days.

All children love to suck the water out of a sponge or flannel; you probably remember doing it yourself. It may be unhygienic, but how do you prevent it? It seems to do no harm.

Once you have got a reluctant child into the bath, persuading him to get out becomes the problem. 'Do you want to pull the plug out, or shall I?' is a ploy that sometimes succeeds. Once the water has run out the child is happy to be enfolded in a warm towel. Our grandchildren like to be wrapped up like a parcel in the towel. Granny or grandpa is the postman and delivers the parcel by dumping it on our bed. Crawlers and toddlers love tumbling about on a double bed, but be alert to prevent them falling off. For the smallest ones, after the bath is a good time to give a baby massage, or allow nappy-free playtime, with the baby lying on a towel on the bed kicking, wriggling and gurgling.

'Sleep that knits up the ravell'd sleave of care'

> *In winter I get up at night*
> *And dress by yellow candlelight.*

> *In summer quite the other way -*
> *I have to go to bed by day.*
> *Bed in Summer*, Robert Louis Stevenson

There is no doubt that sleep is right up there with food and discipline as a Big Issue for parents. It is easy to understand why. We haven't forgotten that when an infant is neither sleeping nor eating, he is almost certainly yelling. And, given that small babies don't know the difference between day and night, he is just as likely to be yelling when his parents are trying to sleep. So the parents have a double worry.

First, they are worried about the baby – is he crying because he is in pain, or upset about something? Secondly they are worried about themselves. How will they ever get enough rest to get them through the next day? The more tired they get, the worse the problem seems. According to research published in the *Times*, in the first four months of a new baby's life, the mum sleeps an average of just four hours each night.

No wonder copious words have been poured into books and articles offering expert advice on the subject. Every childcare manual has a chapter devoted to it and an internet search on 'sleep training' will connect you to thousands of websites. But that is not all. There are dozens of books with titles like *Sleeping Through the Night*, *The No-cry Sleep Solution*, and *The Sleep Book for Tired Parents*.

Sleep training often involves the sinisterly named technique of 'controlled crying'. I remember doing something like it, some 40 years ago. I let my daughter cry for most of the night, having convinced myself that she was 'playing up'. In the morning a bright, pearly new tooth had appeared. I still feel guilty. My philosophy is now, and should have been then, never to harden your heart in matters of childcare. My readers may not feel the same way, and we should respect each other's different ideas. Our attitude to bringing up a family is formed by our own personality, as well as our experience.

GRANNIES SAY:
They stay up later with me. At home they go to bed promptly, same time every day. I rarely manage this.

They go to bed when asked, with us.

I'm more lax about this. Their parents are dead strict.

They tend to go to bed all right, but not to want to stay there.

Being read to helps and my granddaughter has a great

little machine that plays a story tape whilst making a pattern of light on the ceiling and then turns itself off. This seems to work for her.

Bedtime by 7pm if possible.

Bedtime tends to be extended and I get very tired.

They have an excellent regime which I follow.

MUMS SAY:
Whatever suits granny best is OK with me.

Bedtime routine is vitally important to me and I really don't want to have to re-establish it just because grandparents think it's OK to muck it around.

Babies, and sometimes quite senior toddlers, usually have a bottle last thing before bed, then it is time to tuck them up. Sing your lullaby, if that is part of the routine, then tiptoe out of the room murmuring reassuringly, with your fingers crossed.

With toddlers the final stages of bedtime take a little longer. Our toddler grandchildren like to play 'running' after their bath and before putting on their pyjamas. There is a long corridor in our house and the door to our bedroom is at one end. The grandparent sits on the bed with the door open and each child in turn scampers the length of the passage, gathering speed until he flings him-self into the grandparent's arms. The children never seem to doubt for a moment that they will be safely caught and held. The older and bigger they get the more hazardous this is for the adult. If you wear glasses, take them off first. I know they are supposed to have a quiet time before bed, but they have such fun with this game that I make the excuse that letting off steam exhausts them so they are finally ready for sleep.

Once upon a time… the bedtime story

Phew, in bed at last. The gin-and-tonic is getting closer. Or is it? You hope that, like the Flopsy Bunnies after eat-ing too much lettuce, your grandchildren will be soporif-ic. But before they finally fall asleep they must have story time.

Children as young as one year old enjoy the routine of a bedtime story. It helps them to wind down, and they like to cuddle up with you, look at the pictures and help you turn the pages of a board book. It will not be long before they like listening to a simple narrative. By the time they have started at primary school some children will read the odd word to you, partly from memory and partly because they have begun to recognise words.

Make reading the bedtime story the last thing on the

agenda, after brushing teeth and going to the loo. Ideally your grandchild should be snuggled up in bed when you read, with no excuse to get out again. But if the family have a different routine, stick to that. When there are two children of different ages in the same bedroom, we each read a different story to one of the children and it somehow works.

It's best if the child chooses the book, then it won't bore him or be too scary. Annoyingly, children usually reject the new book you brought as a present, insisting on an old favourite. Children seem never to tire of seeing and hearing the same story night after night after night. But you certainly will, and you may find it convenient to lose certain books when they have been around for a while.

I used to try and interest my grandchildren in stories that I knew when I was little, and that I had read to their parents, but *Peter Rabbit* and *Squirrel Nutkin* are not every modern child's cup of tea. It is reassuring to find that *Thomas the Tank Engine*, *The Wind in the Willows*, *Winnie the Pooh* and *The Jungle Book* have survived, albeit in dumbed down or Disney-ized versions. *The Tiger who Came to Tea* and *Where the Wild Things Are* have stayed popular for two generations, and modern books that are a success with grannies as well as children include *Bear*

Hunt, *The Gruffalo*, *The Very Hungry Caterpillar* and *Owl Babies*. For other modern books that seem to have staying power and may not be familiar to you, see the list on page 347.

Our grandchildren think it hilarious when grandpa deliberately 'reads' the wrong words, for example, 'Hey diddle diddle, the cat had a piddle.'

> *Night night, sleep tight*
> *Mind the fleas don't bite*

When grandchildren stay with you, stick to the same arrangements they have at home as far as lights on or off and door open or shut are concerned. If fear of the dark is a problem they may be used to a night light in their room. When I was a child a night light was what now seems to be known as a 'tea light', that is to say, a stubby candle, which burns for a long time. Sometimes the wick was still alight in a pool of molten wax when I woke up next morning. Nowadays it would be considered a terrible fire hazard. Modern night lights are electric and a good deal safer. To some extent one can anticipate minor fears that might keep children awake. When toddlers have recently graduated from a cot to a bed, they may be afraid of falling out, especially if it has happened before. You can put a mattress or cushions on the floor by the bed, or you can simply let them sleep on a mattress on the floor.

If your grandchild is in the throes of toilet training, he may be afraid of wetting the bed. Put a waterproof sheet or pad on the bed and reassure him that it really doesn't matter if he pees in his sleep. If he is used to peeing in a potty, make sure he knows there is one by his bed.

After you have said 'good night' be firm. Easier said than done, I know, and I find it hard to practise what I preach, but if you respond to calls for trivial reasons, you are making a stick to beat yourself. Go right away, pour yourself that stiff drink you were looking forward to, and keep an ear tuned to the monitor if you use one.

The children are probably as tired as you are and initial grizzling, or even crying, usually subsides quickly, provided you do not disturb the peace yourselves by noisy chat and laughter or turning up the volume of the radio or television in a room immediately below them. Of course, if you hear sounds of real distress, you will respond.

Disturbed nights

> Hush, little baby, don't say a word
> Mama's gonna buy you a mockin' bird.

If that mockin' bird don't sing
Mama's gonna buy you a diamond ring

Children who regularly keep their parents awake at night because they are themselves unable to sleep cause great anguish. It is important to know that babies and small children get as much sleep as they need, if not at night, then partly during the day. It is the parents who suffer, and the grandparents too, when they are in charge.

What do you do when your grandchild wakes in the night and won't settle down? If it is a request for a drink of water or for the light to be left on, you can comply. Don't miss the opportunity to take her to the loo, offer the potty or change the nappy. This may help her to settle.

If she seems distressed or homesick, it may help to sit by the bed and stroke her head gently, saying soothing words or singing a gentle lullaby. The general consensus among practitioners of sleep training is, however often you feel the need to go into a sleepless child's room to reassure her, you should never take a baby out of her cot or a toddler out of her bed.

You may find yourself having to answer the question 'Can I come in your bed, granny?' from a child who will not settle at bedtime, or who wakes in the night. When we were bringing up our children it was considered a bad idea, but now, although some childcare experts (including the popular Gina Ford who advocates strict routine) think it unwise, co-sleeping, as it is called, is no longer considered a crime.

Some nursing mothers take their babies into bed with them to make the night-time feed easier, and, once started, the habit is hard to break, with the result that many children are used to cuddling up with their parents from a very early age.

Six per cent of three-year-olds in the UK sleep regularly in their parents' beds. In many cultures it has always been the norm and according to *The Great Ormond Street New Baby and Child Care Book*, 'If you do not mind, then it is not a problem, however unorthodox it might seem to another family.'

Whether you let your grandchild come into your bed depends partly on whether he is used to sleeping with his parents at home. But mostly it depends on your own inclination. On the whole, our generation disapproves of co-sleeping, perhaps simply because we didn't do it ourselves. Your own sleep pattern will certainly be disrupted with a child in bed with you, so you may want to refuse. But there is a compromise open to you. 'Yes,' you might say, 'you can go to sleep in my bed, and when you have gone to sleep I will put you back in your own bed without waking you up.' One of my grandsons, when he was two and three, simply would not settle unless I got into his bed with him and stayed there until he was asleep. At home one or other of his parents always did this, so I did it too.

The sleeping arrangements of older children are likely to be outside your control, and they may be used to staying up as late as they wish at home. However, it should be possible, for your own peace of mind, to establish a rule that they go to bed when you do. This means they won't be watching 'unsuitable' programmes on television or logging onto unsuitable websites. You can't force them to go to sleep, but during the holidays there is no reason they shouldn't read in bed for as long as they like.

Sweet dreams.

The morning after

Morning has broken like the first morning
Blackbird has spoken like the first bird.

However appealing the little pyjama-ed figure clutching a teddy and trailing a comfort blanket may be, you will not feel like welcoming it warmly at 6am. With a bit of luck it can be coaxed back to its own bed, and may even go back to sleep for an hour. But the chances of you and your co-grandparent getting any more sleep are slim. In order to pre-empt this situation, I strongly recommend investing in light-excluding window blinds. I calculate the average gain as 30 minutes in each 24 hours.

MUMS SAY:
I wish she would offer her help in the mornings when she comes to stay so that we could catch up on some sleep.

I love it when they look after them first thing in the morning so we can stay in bed.

'Little' Granny died when I was quite young, but I have fond memories of cuddles in her bed in the morning when she came to stay, and her saying 'mind my corns'.

From the age of four or five onwards, you can set rules about what time they are allowed to wake you. If you put an alarm clock in their room you can set it to the time you want, and impress upon them that they must stay quietly in their room playing or reading until it rings. The downside of that arrangement is that, if the alarm did not go off, they might, by some miracle, have slept or remained quiet for half an hour longer, to everyone's benefit. The way round this, assuming they cannot yet tell the time, is to switch off the alarm but mark the clock with nail varnish, putting a big spot on, for example, the 6 to show where the big hand should be and a small spot for the little hand between the 7 and the 8. This will show them where the hands should be at half past seven. If they sleep beyond that time, so much the better. You can too.

At weekends, having grandchildren in your bed for a before-breakfast cuddle is a treat. Alas, ours are soon bored with cuddling and trot off to chase the cat or fetch a book to be read sitting up in bed. Then it is breakfast time, then time to get dressed. Occasionally, if we are all feeling decadent, they are allowed, still wearing dressing gowns and slippers, to watch Children's TV or a video. If the parents are also staying with you, the objective is to make this part of the day last as long as possible, so as to prolong their lie-in. Breakfast can be spun out by getting the children to lay the table, spread their own toast with butter and marmite, and put the plates in the dishwasher when they have finished. Getting dressed lasts twice as long if they dress themselves and have to find the missing sock themselves. Anything put on back to front has to be taken off and put on again.

On weekdays during term-time, when you are looking after your grandchildren at their own house, the reverse applies. Time is of the essence. You have to get them up, fed, dressed in the right clothes and to school on time, so speed and efficiency are called for.

A less traumatic time will be had by all if you remember to put out their clothes the night before, and leave ready their schoolbags, PE kit and anything else that is required. If your grandchildren are dawdlers or daydreamers, allow extra time. Even if they normally dress themselves, you may find it easier to help out when time is short – provided they'll let you. Reluctant children often respond if you make a game of it, pretending you can't find their vest or sock, or you think their shirt buttons up at the back.

When you are looking after older, teenage grandchildren, the difficult part is to get them out of bed in time to eat any breakfast at all before they dash out of the house. They are probably conditioned to sleep through their alarm, so you will just have to give them a good shake every five or ten minutes until they respond.

Your quality moment finally arrives when you can sit down at the kitchen table with a fresh cup of coffee and the newspaper.

CHAPTER 11 – DISCIPLINE

There was a little girl who had a little curl,
Right in the middle of her forehead.
When she was good, she was very, very good,
But when she was bad she was horrid.

Henry Wadsworth Longfellow

I hope this is going to be a short, sharp chapter. The question of discipline is a minefield I was tempted to leave unexplored. But there is no doubt that it can be a Big Issue between parents and grandparents. Under the general heading of 'discipline' there are some potentially difficult problems to be faced. There is the question of whether, if you think the parents are going about it all wrong, you should speak out, and whether, when you have your grandchildren to yourself, you are justified in applying your own forms of discipline.

Although there are plenty of exceptions to the rule, the pendulum of discipline seems to swing between permissiveness and strictness from one generation to the next, within a general framework of increased permissiveness.

The majority of grandparents think their grandchildren's parents are not strict enough. Today's parents love to explain the reasons for their decisions; 'because I say so' is a phrase that does not spring to their lips as readily as it did to ours. On the other hand, most of us also love the way parents can talk to their children so frankly and openly, and are so interested in their opinions. It seems you can't have it both ways.

GRANNIES SAY:
With our formidable grandmother relations were formal rather than close.

My mother treated her mother as if she were the Queen and expected us to do the same. They were both frozen in time.

My grandmother was very loving but would stand no nonsense.

Granny was very strict – we were scared of her!

Very much a disciplinarian, very little fun.

My mum always felt the need to clean the house before granny arrived; and insisted we behave unnaturally well in her presence because, presumably, it reflected on her parenting skills.

'Spare the rod and spoil the child'

I knew both my grandmothers and learnt from them something of what it was like to be a child in the 1890s. My own grandchildren are growing up in the 2000s. So, without any exceptional feats of longevity in the family, I have knowledge of five generations (my grandmother, my mother, myself, my daughter and my grandchildren) spanning more than a century. As far as discipline is concerned, I know that my grandmother and my mother were brought up strictly, in a system where bad behaviour was punished rather than good behaviour rewarded. My mother's way of bringing up her children was more easy-going but I think this was due to her character rather than to the childcare fashion of the day. I don't remember any smacks from her. For serious naughtiness she, in common with many other mothers of her generation, would issue the threat 'wait till your father gets home': a way of dealing with the situation that is unthinkable to most civilised parents today, making the father into a monster who delivers violent retribution (in the case of my brother and me, administered, not very hard, with the back of a hairbrush on a bare bottom). It was a rare occurrence and, although I can remember the punishment after all these years, I have no idea what the crime was.

My own children were born in the permissive 1960s, and I was a fairly permissive mother. When they were babies, after a flirtation with Dr Spock, I fed them on demand, and later we paid little attention to fixed mealtimes or bedtime. We spent much more time doing things with our children than my parents' generation had. Looking back, I can see that we spoiled them, but they seem to have turned out well in spite of that.

Judging from the way our children and their friends bring up their children, routine is back in vogue in many families. Gina Ford, whose name I have already mentioned in several contexts (though not as frequently as the parents of our grandchildren mention it), is today's fashionable equivalent to Dr Spock. Her books the *Contented Little Baby Book* and *From Contented Baby to Confident Child* are bestsellers. Gina Ford's methods are based on the premise that babies and children do better within the structure of a strict routine, closer to the way

I was brought up than to the way I brought up my own children. To implement the routine she advocates requires a fairly robust attitude to discipline on the part of the parents, and I am watching with interest to see how well her methods work.

Getting it right

We can divide discipline into two broad categories: one is the maintenance of an orderly routine, making daily life comfortable and enjoyable for both children and grown-ups; the other is to do with one-off incidents of naughtiness and how to deal with them. It goes without saying that, hard as it is to keep your lip buttoned when you think the parents are meting out unfair punishments or letting the children get away with murder, the Good Granny should follow the guidance of the parents about what is and is not allowed, rather than developing theories of her own.

GRANNIES SAY:
His manners are better when his mother is not there.

I admire the way the parents try to control and guide the children without relying on heavy discipline.

The parents are MUCH less strict than we were.

I am sorry not to be able to 'spoil' the grandchildren. Annoyingly it goes against the grain. Not because they are spoilt already, but more because it is so contrary to the way I feel children should be brought up – granny shouldn't be loved as the bearer of gifts.

MUMS SAY:
When I try to discipline my daughter, my mother-in-law unhelpfully contradicts me – 'If you don't apologise to granny for biting her, no sweets' I say, and she steps in, 'Oh no, of course she can have them.'

They never have tantrums with granny – only us.

When children are difficult, their grandparents have a better chance than their parents of getting them to behave reasonably, simply because children have an on-going agenda of testing and challenging parental authority, to see how far they can push the boundaries. Many parents find this hard to handle, but you, the granny, have no history of confrontation in your relationship, nor do you have to deal with the problems day in, day out. One granny looks after her two grandchildren while their mum works part-time, and their mum admits that she has more influence over their behaviour than either parent.

It is not universally true that grandparents love to indulge their grandchildren. Some of us feel nothing but irritation when we find we can't walk past the sweet shop or the ice-cream van without being wheedled to buy a treat. I come across plenty of grandparents who think that it is the parents who spoil the children – working mothers often carry a burden of guilt towards their children, for example, which manifests itself as a relaxation of discipline – so they try unobtrusively to do what they can to redress the balance, introducing a degree of routine and discipline into their grandchildren's lives whenever they get the chance.

Everyday problems

Rudeness, lack of respect for elders and betters, including their parents, and bad manners come high on this list. Several of the grannies I know get particularly heated about their grandchildren's table manners. Another thinks they are bad at greeting people and saying goodbye. One granny feels very strongly on the subject: 'It is fundamental to children's upbringing. A rude child is a selfish and unfeeling person – which of course we all basically are – but, our whole humanity rests on our control of how we behave towards others.'

Unacceptable everyday behaviour from a granny's

point of view includes extreme untidiness; not listening; noisiness (and squealing, grizzling); fighting or running around the house; being silly; and staying up too late, 'should be 7 but it's 10'. 'Sometimes', a granny writes, 'they are very greedy and want anything they can get out of you (toys/money/sweets).'

Dealing with the problems

How does the Good Granny ensure that all is sweetness and light when she is in charge? If your grandchildren's home life is, in your judgement, too confrontational, then a non-confrontational approach will probably work wonders in your house. Be watchful, anticipate trouble and head it off using distraction tactics. Keeping children fully occupied doing things they enjoy leaves them no time to be a nuisance or get into trouble. Say 'Goodness gracious, it's time to water the garden.' Or post a letter, or take the dog for a walk.

Mild forms of bad behaviour such as rudeness, sulking because he can't have what he wants, refusing to do as he is told, or persistently and deliberately annoying you (by kicking a table leg, for example) are best ignored. Look away (this is called 'withdrawing eye contact' by child-care experts), walk off and start doing something else. If that doesn't work, go right out of the room, shutting the door behind you. When you come back, assume that the bad moment has passed and talk happily about something completely different.

Dawdling can be extremely irritating, indoors or out, deliberate or unconscious. Try setting an example by being brisk in your actions and tone of voice. If that fails, offer a bribe: 'You can watch television for ten minutes before school if you get dressed quickly'; 'We'll have ice-cream for tea if we get home by five o'clock.'

Grannies say:
It's the whinging that really gets to me. But they only do it when Mum or Dad are around.

Be firm. Tone of voice matters. I say 'No more of that' then ignore

The little one whinges: I think the youngest in a family always does – I think she should be treated with the same firmness that the older one is.

Whinging is not to be tolerated. First, listen carefully: are they actually miserable, frightened, confused? Children do sometimes whinge because they are tired, hungry, thirsty, too cold or too hot, or unhappy for one reason or another. More often, they whinge because it worked for them last time. 'I want,' said in a whiney enough voice, often enough, finally breaks the parents' patience — hard as they try to insist that 'no' means 'no', their toddler knows better. 'No' comes to mean 'I'm saying "no" now, but if you go on whinging long enough I'll change my mind and say "all right then, just this once."'

You, granny, have a chance to wipe the slate clean by standing firm come what may. It is never too early to teach that no means no, and granny and grandpa are not a soft touch. A Good Granny's advice is to tell your grandchild you can't understand her when she speaks in a whiney voice. She must speak properly if she wants you to listen. If she goes on whinging, say 'I can't hear you' and ignore her and avoid eye contact until she speaks normally. You may have to repeat the process frequently before you get the desired effect.

Granny's Finger

A great friend of mine and one of the most devoted grannies you could ever meet, with a great fund of common sense, relied on 'Granny's Finger' to control her unruly mob of five grandchildren. Her index finger, held upright in silence, was the equivalent of a football referee's yellow-card. It stopped the offender in his tracks and, if he should launch into a protest or explanation,

Granny's Finger would be lifted a couple of inches higher and the expression on her face would grow more serious. It always worked for her.

Bad behaviour, and how to deal with it

> *Tom, Tom the Piper's son*
> *Stole a pig and away he ran.*
> *The pig was eat and Tom was beat*
> *And Tom went roaring down the street.*

What about more serious problems? How can you deal with behaviour that is disruptive to other children or to adults? If your badly behaved grandchild's parents are not around to deal with the problem, it becomes your problem, and you have to decide whether to go for the stick or the carrot, or a bit of both. My first rule is to remove the offender from the scene, either into another room, or if you are outdoors, out of earshot. You are more likely to get a positive response one to one, without an audience to play to. I remember an occasion in our garden when a four-year-old boy persistently spoiled the other children's games, behaving aggressively, lashing out at another child, really trying to hurt him. Such a child is clearly not happy, and is almost certainly not going to respond to reasoning from his parents.

Grandparents have a slightly better chance, so I thought I would have a go. I took him round the corner, out of sight, held his arm firmly, and made him look at me. Then, talking quietly in a friendly tone, I impressed upon him that no one would want to play with him if he went round kicking them. Did he understand?

It is important to get an answer to this. You just have to persist gently until you do. Then reward him with a hug and return to the group. Just having full attention, one to one, in a grown-up way, seems to make a difference. For the rest of the afternoon he played happily with the other children.

The terrible twos

Is it tempting providence to say that the awfulness of two-year-olds is exaggerated? It is true they can shout at you, run away from you, hit and kick you, squirm out of your hold, out of the buggy, out of the car seat. You need to be physically strong, and this is the age when you may be tempted to deliver a short, sharp smack. It seems as if grandparents find it hard to resist the temptation; 75% of the grandparents questioned in a recent survey didn't think it should be illegal for a grandparent to smack a grandchild (smacking by anyone including parents is illegal in some countries).

Almost certainly your grandchildren's parents will have a no-smacking rule and if you break it they may never trust you in the same way again. They may even stop you looking after the child on your own. That said, if you do give way to the smacking impulse, it's best to own up. If you don't, your grandchild will almost certainly sneak on you. Imagine the shame of hearing the words, loud and clear, out of the mouth of a babe, 'Granny smacked me' or, worse still, 'Granny hit me.'

> *'I'll thcream and I'll thcream and I'll thcream
> till I'm thick'*
> Violet-Elizabeth Bott in *Just William*,
> Richmal Crompton

Out-and-out tantrums are most likely to occur during the terrible twos, but they can happen at any age (18% of three-year-olds still have at least one tantrum a day), and are horribly unnerving. A tantrum usually comes suddenly, out of nowhere, as an apparently completely irrational over-reaction to some minor frustration. It is quite likely to happen, embarrassingly, in a public place.

We have all seen a desperate parent at the supermarket checkout, with a purple-faced child screaming blue murder. The parent may lose control and start yelling back at the child, and may lash out with a desperate, instinctive smack. None of this does any good. The tantrum continues unabated. If it happens to you, your best course is to pick up the child and remove it from the scene. Not so easy if you are halfway through your trans actions at the checkout; you may have to leave your grandchild lying on the ground screaming, while you finish. He has probably gone rigid, so all you can do is then clamp him firmly under one arm like a surfboard, while you push your laden trolley to the car with the other. Definitely not a situation the little old granny with the grey bun and the cardigan could cope with. But we are made of sterner stuff.

GRANNIES SAY:
Tantrums are rare but hell. You can't lift them up as they go stiff!!

The parents are often not brave enough to weather the storm.

Don't give in to blackmail.

If it is for no other reason than they can't get what they want, and I can't get them to stop with reasoning, I put them in the bedroom to calm down – popping in several times just to check they're OK.

Most grannies recommend putting the child in her room to cool off. But one granny claims with pride, 'Only once ever in 12 years have I sent one to her room.' A short period of isolation, referred to as 'Time Out', is recommended in many child-care books. One granny suggests a very short sentence of Time Out for very small offenders: 'Sit the child on the bottom of stairs for 30 seconds, then retrieve and praise fulsomely.'

This is quite a well-known method, the bottom stair being known as 'the naughty step'. I like the idea suggested by a compassionate granny, of giving the naughty one an egg timer. When the sand has run out, she can come back. I did come across one smacking granny, who said she would smack first and tell the parents after, but the vast majority go for the soft approach:

GRANNIES SAY:
Try and calm the child with strokes and comforting words, then cuddle it when the tantrum is over. It won't

last long. It's usually because they're tired or hungry.

Encourage the child to look at you, then mirror their expression and gradually change yours to a smile and gentle laugh.

We've been through tantrums: I pretend it's not happening and my grandson gets bored. Sometimes I will go out of the room for a moment then come back and suggest something nice to do, like go out to the park.

A child having a tantrum is not being deliberately naughty or trying to annoy you. He has just completely lost the plot. You can sometimes tell by listening to the tone of the relentless bawling whether the tantrum stems from anger, jealousy, fear or frustration, or all of these. The anguish expressed can be heartbreaking, and it is difficult not to burst into tears in sympathy. It is distressing for you not to be able to make it better with a kiss and a cuddle, but usually the tantrum has to run its course. Some children are comforted if you get hold of them and hug them very close and tight until the storm has passed, and the bellowing has subsided into hiccups. At this stage, washing the child's face with cool water, followed by a drink of water, has a soothing effect.

General principles

In this chapter I have looked at worst-case scenarios. Luckily, most of the time children and their grandparents are enjoying each other's company too much for discipline to be an issue at all. And the parents I have come across seem to be broadly supportive of granny's 'old-fashioned' approach to manners and behaviour.

Twenty-first-century parents tend to remember their own grandparents as people to look up to, with exemplary manners. If they had 'bossy ways' these were recalled with affection, and although good behaviour was required, this didn't prevent a close and loving relationship. It is perhaps salutary to remember that, if we regard our children and grandchildren as less strict or less respectful than our generation, in truth it is not they who fail to meet our standards but we who allowed, and even encouraged, the standards to change.

One of my mother's few rules was 'What you have promised, you must perform,' as the King said to his daughter in *The Frog Prince*. This is an important rule from a child's point of view, and slightly easier for grandparents to observe than for parents, because we have more time. 'Not now, I'm too busy' may be a necessary answer from a parent, but a granny can do better than that. If it is sometimes hard to keep promises of puppies, presents, and treats, it is even harder, but still necessary, to carry out threats. What if you are foolish enough to say, 'If you don't come and have your lunch NOW, I won't take you to the circus'? What you have promised, you must per- form. And don't expect a handsome prince disguised as a frog to come to your aid.

Instead of a threat, the best response to bad behaviour is often to see the funny side. If you laugh, the child may be taken unawares and laugh back. Nobody, child or adult, can keep up a sulk or a whinge when they are laughing.

Finally, the parents do not want to hear you say 'I can't understand it – she's always good as gold with me.' They need all the praise you can give, to boost their confi- dence, so do let them know if you think they are doing a good job bringing up your grandchildren, and *tell* them if you think the children are polite, happy, cheerful and fun to be with.

PART IV – **WHEN THINGS GO WRONG**

Grandparenthood, and family life in general, cannot be unalloyed happiness, and this book aims to cover the bad times as well as the good. The support of grandparents has never been so much needed as it is now, in sickness as well as in health, when separation and divorce occur, and when families suffer bereavement. This chapter suggests ways you can help at such times of grave crisis as well as with more everyday problems.

CHAPTER 12 – WHEN THINGS GO WRONG
FOR THE CHILDREN

New baby syndrome: sympathy for siblings
The happiness grandparents experience when their first

grandchild is born will, with a bit of luck, be repeated in due course. Some grandparents have a passion for new-born babies. Such baby-worshippers, as we may call them, find themselves, when each new grandchild comes along, instinctively transferring their full attention, and indeed their total adoration, to the new arrival. The new baby's parents and siblings are, of course, not happy about this. A mother whose sister-in-law has just had a baby writes, 'My parents have now got a new grandchild and all of a sudden they don't have any time for our daughter who was the first grandchild and who they used to love so much.' Another mum complains that her mother-in-law 'never offers to help, just takes the current baby on her lap and coos inanely at it for the duration of the visit.'

It is a problem recognised by Dr Spock who wrote, 'A grandmother or other care-giver may favour the youngest child in the family... she may call that one "Granny's Baby". If she can't understand the harm in doing this, she should not stay.'

Inevitably a new baby is going to take up a lot of the parents' time, so that less time is available for older children. Plenty of advice is on offer elsewhere about how to deal with this and how to introduce an older brother or sister to the new baby, but few of the books recognise that grandparents can play an important role. First of all, you can make sure you give extra time and demonstrate special affection to the older sibling.

That said, there is a balance to be struck: it may seem natural to you to offer to have the older child, who knows and loves you, to stay with you for a few days, allowing the parents to concentrate on the baby. But however much the older grandchild loves you, if he is sent to stay with you, he may feel his parents are excluding him, and he will blame the baby for it. Sometimes it is best to offer your service at his house – to take charge of the baby in between feeds, giving the parents quality time with the older child.

Your older grandchild will be grateful if you refrain from bombarding him with questions about the new baby. Leave others to say, 'What do you think of your little sister?' as they surely will or, worse, 'Do you love your little sister?' Your job is to reassure your grandchild that, in spite of the interloper, he is still the centre of your universe.

Occasionally a toddler may show extreme jealousy of the new baby, trying to push it off his mother's lap when she is breastfeeding, and trying to hurt the baby when he thinks no one is looking. The mother is already finding it hard to fulfil the needs of the new baby as well as those of a stroppy toddler. Her hormones are causing her emotions to see-saw and she is almost certainly suffering from exhaustion. With the first baby, she could grab a nap when the baby slept, but now there are two, the opportunity just doesn't arise. A jealous older child threatening the baby becomes a threat to her own sanity. Step in, Good Granny, and rescue her. In the crucial first few weeks, give as much help as you can with housework, cooking, laundry. Spread an atmosphere of calm.

Favouritism

MUMS SAY:

Although all their grandparents and step-grandparents are very different, the children react to them all with equal and very great affection. It particularly amazes me that they do not notice how annoying and bizarre my mother-in-law is.

I have found it remarkable how my children have found their own level with both sets of grandparents. My parents love being actively involved in all aspects of their upbringing whereas my in-laws are quite the opposite, but the children talk of them with the same emotion and love, and concern when they are ill. Children obviously don't have the same hang-ups as adults and this is a good lesson to me!

GRANNIES SAY:
I do have a favourite grandchild but I hope I never show it – I feel rather ashamed about it, but nevertheless it's inside me privately.

It's inevitable, I love them all the same but there's always going to be one special one.

I don't have a favourite; they are all very precious to me.

Most of the grannies I have talked to admit that, whilst all their grandchildren are beloved, they have a best beloved, and this is confirmed by most mums. For some grandparents the first grandchild will always be special. For those who are incurable baby-worshippers, it is always the youngest.

Parents and grandparents all agree that it is unforgivable to let it be seen that you have a favourite, but, from the comments of some mums, it seems we do not always succeed in hiding our partiality as well as we should.

MUMS SAY:
My mother-in-law has a favourite son and therefore favours his children. As a mother one cannot possibly come to terms with the fact that a family member loves

someone else's children more than your own. And of course the children don't understand. It's very, very sad.

My mother had an un-favourite grandchild – adopted and the wrong (from mum's point of view) racial mix. She was very unkind both to and about this poor child.

My mother-in-law loved spoiling the two older girls, buying smocked dresses and Peter Rabbit books, but was positively unpleasant to my youngest who was stout and wore thick glasses.

Mum tends to favour the cuddly, smiley toddler at the expense of my older daughter who is much more prickly.

My gran definitely and publicly had favourites among the grandchildren. I wasn't one and this hurt.

Don't get me started!!! Favouritism is rife in our family and the cause of a lot of problems.

Good Grannies will be aware of the dangers of favouritism, and take steps to avoid them. It is clearly wrong to single out one child for special attention in the way of extra presents or outings, and easy enough to avoid. However, you may not even be aware that, when you are all together, you pay more attention to your favourite, laugh more at how cute she is, sit her next to you at meal times, and let her whisper secrets in your ear. All this can be distressing for less favoured siblings.

Conversely, if you find one of your grandchildren more irritating and less attractive than the others (and it is only human to feel like this), do be aware of the upset you may cause by showing it. Although you may be careful enough never consciously to pick on this child, unconsciously you may be transmitting negative messages to or about him. The easiest way to be even-handed is to have each child to stay, or take each one out, on her own from time to time, as I have suggested in other contexts. With your best beloved out of the way, you are less likely to make unfavourable comparisons, and what you perceive as the shortcomings of the merely beloved will be less obvious. By spending time one-to-one you can build a closer relationship, and arrive at an understanding of your grandchild, getting her to talk to you about any problems that may be the root cause of her irritating behaviour.

Illness

Now that so many mums are at work, and their childcare arrangements are delicately balanced, even quite minor ailments can be disruptive. On days when a child has to be kept home from school, playgroup or nursery because of a sore throat or earache, the first thing many mums do is, send for Supergran. Gran, if she really is Super, cancels her tennis lesson, postpones wallpapering the spare room, drops everything and comes.

GRANNIES SAY:
We helped our daughter and son-in-law last year when my grandson badly broke his arm in two places, by being there for his younger brother, while they spent time in the hospital, and he came to us when his mum and dad went back to work.

The first time I looked after my granddaughter on her own I took her for a walk and when we got home and I unzipped her from her snowsuit I found she was covered in spots – German Measles. The second time, she had a serious choke on a grape and I had to hold her by her feet and shake her until it shot out; a nasty moment.

A Doctor came hurrying round, and he said:
"Tut-tut, I am sorry to find you in bed.
Just say "Ninety-nine", while I look at your chest...
Don't you find that chrysanthemums answer the best?"
The Dormouse and the Doctor, A.A. Milne

The care of small patients has changed since we were children. If one's temperature was above 'normal' one had to stay in bed, with a glass of lucozade and mum's portable wireless on the bedside table. If the temperature went above 100 degrees, the doctor was summoned.

As well as listening to your chest he would inspect your tongue, and peer into your throat ('Say aah!'). There was no question of getting up and coming downstairs until your temperature had been normal for 24 hours. Once up and dressed, another day followed doing jigsaw puzzles or colouring before you were allowed outdoors. Granny sometimes came, to read a story, pop out for Ribena, Lucozade and knitting wool, cast on stitches, and generally be a ministering angel.

Nourishment for sick children took the form of a little boiled fish, minced chicken or a soft-boiled egg. Rice pudding to follow. The Tonic, prescribed to aid recovery and restore the child's strength, might be Parish's Food (reddish brown and disgusting), Angier's Emulsion (sickly green and disgusting), Haliborange (a mixture of concentrated orange juice and halibut-liver-oil – sick-making) or Radio Malt (delicious liquid toffee).

After any more serious illness, such as mumps, measles, prolonged flu' or bronchitis, a spell of convalescence in fresh country air was recommended. In my family that meant a week of pure pleasure at our grandparents' farm. Sometimes sea air was prescribed, and I remember being taken by my grandmother to Lynmouth in Devon. It was early spring and there was no question of bathing or even paddling. We walked on the beach every day, breathing the air deeply.

Now things are different. There is virtually no question of a house call from a doctor, and parents and grandparents are naturally very reluctant to take an ill child to a surgery waiting room full of people coughing and sneezing their germs around. The only reasons to visit the doctor are if the child has unfamiliar symptoms or if you think he needs antibiotics or other prescription-only medicines. If it is difficult to visit the doctor – if there are other children to be looked after, for example – and you are worried, you ring the helpline NHS Direct.

Poorly children with a slight fever and, perhaps, a sore throat, cough or earache are usually just tucked up on the sofa with cushions and duvet, in front of the television and, at the parents' or grandparents' discretion, dosed with Calpol or Baby Nurofen. You can alternate doses of these two medicines. If they are well enough to eat, fish fingers and tomato ketchup will do very well. On the whole, the less fuss made of them, the parents are likely to think, the better. You don't want them enjoying bad health, you want them back at school. Nevertheless, grannies may well seize the opportunity to spoil them a bit. When they are ill, children tend to regress, and, depending on just how ill they are, may like to be treated as babies again. That will suit many grannies, regretting, as they do, the speed at which their grandchildren grow up and away from them.

Just a spoonful of sugar helps the medicine go down
In a most delightful way.

Mary Poppins

Granny, the Wise Woman, may be able to work her healing magic on a child who is under the weather but not seriously ill. Just the idea that granny's lotions and potions are effective may make the child feel better. You can persuade her that something special is happening by mixing her bedtime drink in 'granny's special cup' or glass, and stirring granny's special jam or honey in to sweeten the medicine. It's the way you go about it that counts.

If an illness lasts more than a few days, and there are other children in the family, one of the things a Good Granny can do is make sure they are not neglected. It is only too easy for them to feel resentful of all the attention the sick child is getting while they are left to fend for themselves. You may have to deal with a situation where the well child complains of a tummy ache, headache or sore throat because he wants to stay at home like his sick sister. It is one of the rare occasions when bribery is permissible in the form of an incentive to the well child to go to school without a fuss.

Ill children often have disturbed nights, and if you are staying in the house you will earn undying gratitude if you volunteer as 'night nurse' so the parents can sleep uninterrupted, especially if they both have to go to work the next day. If your grandchild is so fretful that only Mum will do at night, you may be able to give her time off from the sickroom during the day, so she can have a nap.

If your grandchild has to be in hospital, you will naturally want to visit as often as you can, but you will probably be more useful holding the fort at your daughter's or son's house, caring for their other children. If there is advance notice of the hospital visit, you may be able to help prepare your grandchild by playing games of 'doctors and nurses'.

Special needs

It is sad for grandparents as well as parents when the beautiful, intelligent and talented child that they have hoped for turns out to have special physical, mental or emotional problems. But however shattered they feel when they learn of a grandchild's disability, it is far more distressing for the parents. So it is imperative, for their sake and the child's, that grandparents make a conscious effort to overcome their grief and think positively about the situation.

Most grannies belong to a generation of stiff-upper-lippers; we were not brought up to be demonstrative and to share bouts of weeping. This doesn't mean we are unfeeling, it means we are strong. When there is something to be sad about we offer, rather than seek, a shoulder to cry on – and shed our own tears in private.

To help you come to terms with the problem, so that you can be strong for the rest of your family, there are two steps to take that may help. The first is to talk it over, not only with the parents (they have each other), but also with a close friend, if possible someone who has had relevant experience or can put you in touch with such a person.

This is not so difficult as you might think – as many as 20% of children have special needs of one kind or another. You may, initially, be afraid that you will not be able to love the child who is so different. In almost all cases this feeling is temporary, and you will find that your 'different' grandchild has, if anything, a stronger hold on your heartstrings than the others. Whatever your particular anxieties are, sharing them with a friend makes them easier to put in perspective.

The second step is to find out all you can about your grandchild's condition. Once it might have been difficult, but now we can search the internet for reliable and detailed descriptions of such conditions as Attention Deficit Disorder (ADD), Autism, Down's Syndrome and Dyspraxia. Knowledge of the symptoms, the diagnosis and the treatment available for your grandchild's condition can convert despair into hope. The very fact that these conditions are recognised is cause for optimism. A generation ago children suffering from them would have been collectively written off as 'mentally retarded'. Now advice and therapy are available to help the children realise their potential, make sense of the world around them, and find a place in it.

Some disabilities are evident at birth, others become apparent later. Diagnosis can lead to friction between parents and grandparents. One mother complains of her mother adopting an ostrich-like, head-in-the-sand position, fooling herself into thinking that, when her special-needs grandchild behaves unacceptably 'a good smack is all he needs' or 'he will grow out of it'. Parents find this denial hard to forgive at a time when they need all the support they can get. Another mother describes how her parents simply cannot understand her autistic son: 'If he has a meltdown they think he's just being naughty...' By contrast, her mother-in-law 'has taken it all in her stride and really enjoys spending time with him'.

What if the grandparents are the first to suspect that all is not well, or think that they are? The chances are that the parents are also uneasy about their child's develop-ment but they may not be able to acknowledge it, even to each other. 'In denial' is not a phrase that is particular-ly familiar to the granny generation, but it is a useful and accurate phrase in such cases. If your grandchild is show-ing worrying symptoms, and you think she should see a specialist, before you broach the subject to her parents you must be very certain of your facts. Do your home-work. Find out everything you can about whatever dis-order you suspect. If you have a trustworthy friend you can confide in, do so. Even if you yourself don't know or know of a child suffering from that disorder, there is a chance your friend does, and can put you in touch with the parents so you can get first-hand information.

There is no easy, tactful way to tell your grandchild's parents about your fears. One grandmother described how she and her husband agonised for weeks about sug-gesting their son and daughter-in-law should have their grandson tested for autism. They hoped their fears would prove groundless, and that the problem would go away, but their research showed that early diagnosis is important if autistic children are to get the best help, and the grandparents decided they must wait no longer.

'We just took the bull by the horns after dinner with our son and daughter-in-law one night, and came right out with it,' said the granny. 'We tried to be calm and rational and went through a list of his symptoms that worried us. We said that we were probably wrong, and we hoped we were, but why not have the tests to set everyone's minds at rest? It was awful. Our daughter-in-law burst into tears and our son said we were talking rubbish. But I think they knew really, and we were confirming their subconscious fears. They made an appointment with the paediatrician a few days later.'

Loving care at home plays a huge part in building the confidence of special needs children, and that is something good grandparents can supply in abundance. The most constructive way we can express our love is to provide cheerful, practical help. Our ability and willingness to do this may be crucial. Grandparents are among the very few people, other than parents and siblings, who can establish a rapport with a special needs child, and may be the only people the parents trust to take charge and give them a desperately needed break. The better you get to know the child, the more your love will grow. Most special needs children are not unhappy children, quite the contrary, and you will find their happiness infectious and inspiring.

You will find, too, that you, your children and your grandchild are not alone. Before long you will find yourself meeting mothers and fathers, or grandparents of children who have the same problem as your grandchild. They will raise your spirits by telling you how very special that child is to them. They can also help you understand what to expect as your grandchild grows older.

MUMS SAY:
Our elder son is dyspraxic and has other problems, which have never been diagnosed. My mum gave me her complete support from the beginning, when the experts were telling me there was nothing wrong.

My mother was tremendously supportive from the start, and came with us the first time we saw the consultant at Great Ormond Street Hospital.

To begin with my mum was embarrassed and awkward with our Down's syndrome daughter, but now she loves her to bits and they play together very naturally.

A GRANNY SAYS:
Our special needs granddaughter has autism and epilepsy. She brings a degree of chaos into our otherwise smug lives that is both exhausting and liberating.

Sometimes various expensive forms of therapy are recommended for special needs children, and parents cannot always afford to pay for it. Grandparents may be able to help out. One mum said she wished the expensive presents her in-laws showered upon her autistic child could have been converted into therapy. No doubt all she had to do was ask, but she was afraid of offending them. So if you are in this situation, don't wait to be asked – make the offer.

Other problems

As they grow up, your grandchildren will grow away from you. They will form new friendships and have more exciting, absorbing ways to spend their time. Don't have hurt feelings. Instead, be glad they are growing up and finding new interests. It would be odd if a lively ten-year-old wanted to spend all her spare time with an old lady. …Well, if not old, getting on.

If you see less of your grandchildren as they grow up, you can still keep in touch by phone, email or letter, so that they know you are always there for them if they need you. And they may need you at any time. Grandparents can provide a sympathetic ear when there are problems at school, problems with friends, or problems with parents or siblings.

A GRANNY SAYS:
I took the risk of ringing my teenage granddaughter on her mobile after she had a row with her mother. As I didn't come down on her like a ton of bricks but tried to find out gently what had led to the 'scene' she didn't resent my interference, and I think I helped her.

A MUM SAYS:
When my daughter was bullied at school my mother was a good ear and gave her very wise advice, and a safe refuge. She excels in the realm of emotion and was really the one person who understood.

Where to get help

Down's Syndrome Assoc.
0845 230 0372
www.downs-syndrome.org.uk
info@downs-syndrome.org.uk

National Autistic Society
020 7833 2299
www.nas.org.uk
nas@nas.org.uk

The Dyslexia Institute
01784 222300
www.dyslexiaaction.org.uk
info@dyslexiaaction.org.uk

ADD/ADHD support groups
are organised locally.
info@adders.org/englandmap.html

**Assoc. for Spina bifida and
Hydrocephalus**
01733 555988
www.ASBAH.org
info@asbah.org

British Epilepsy Assoc.
0808 800 5050
www.epilepsy.org.uk

Cystic Fibrosis Trust
0208 464 7211

www.cftrust.org.uk
enquiries@cftrust.org.uk

MENCAP National Centre
020 7454 0454
www.mencap.org.uk
information@mencap.org.uk

**National Deaf Children's
Society**
020 7490 8656
www.ndcs.org.uk
ndcs@ndcs.org.uk

**Royal National Institute for
the Blind**
0845 7669999
helpline@rnib.org.uk

SCOPE (Cerebral Palsy Assoc)
020 7619 7100
www.scope.org.uk
cphelpline@scope.org.uk

For help and advice about
other Special Needs problems,
however unusual or rare, try
Contact a Family 020 7608
8700 or 0808 808 3555
www.cafamily.org.uk
info@cafamily.org.uk

CHAPTER 13 – WHEN THINGS GO WRONG
FOR ADULTS

When families suffer unforeseen and perhaps tragic events, grandparents may be the best, perhaps the only, people to take charge. Their courage in adversity and their ability to cope in various unhappy circumstances is truly staggering.

I have come across grandparents who have brought their grandchildren safely through the separation and divorce of their parents, through illness, and through the death of a parent. I know of more than one grandmother who is caring full-time for her grandchildren because their mother is a drug addict, and another who looked after hers whilst both parents served prison sentences. She writes, 'It was very traumatic for all concerned. We counselled the children as best we could (we never tried to turn them against their parents). They are all back together now. We are still involved with our grand-children and we keep an eye on their situation ready to step in if we have to.'

Whatever the sad situation may be, the qualities most needed when things go wrong are calmness, reliability and the practical sense to see what needs doing and do it.

Baby blues

Did mothers of our generation know about Post-Natal Depression (PND), or is it one of those problems that science has revealed and catalogued more recently? Some of us certainly suffered from something known as the 'baby blues'. It was real and could be very debilitating, but you were supposed to overcome it by 'pulling your-self together'. Now it is known that one in ten mothers suffers from PND.

Most mothers get weepy and depressed in the first few weeks. Between the third and seventh day after the birth, as the mother's milk comes in, her hormone levels fluctuate violently, sometimes causing mood swings from elation to tearful depression. The climax of nine months of excited anticipation has happened and is over. Now the new mother is faced with an interminable, and often seemingly thankless task: bringing up baby. If it is her first baby she wonders if she is up to the job. If she has done it before she wonders how she ever got through it last time, and how she will manage to cope with two. I remember being thrilled at the thought of bringing my first baby home from the hospital, then bursting into floods of tears on the threshold of our flat although my wonderful mother-in-law had spring cleaned it and filled it with flowers. It all just seemed too difficult.

It is quite normal for a mother to be weepy for the first six to eight weeks of the baby's life. But if the feeling of depression increases, lasting for longer periods each day, she needs help. As we have already seen, all mothers of newborns are tired most of the time and could do with some mothering themselves. This is where the Good Granny comes in, treading the tightrope between helping and interfering.

In serious cases of PND, granny is justified in getting bossy. People who are depressed can't pull themselves out of it. They are too listless to take the initiative. A depressed mum feels tired, sad, inadequate and without hope for the future. She becomes more and more irritable with the baby and with other people around her, and then suffers deeply from guilt. It is all she can do to get herself up and dressed in the morning, let alone eat and sleep properly, and get out of the house from time to time. If you think it may be necessary, talk her into seeing her GP (take her to the surgery yourself) or make sure you are with her when the health visitor calls.

At the very least, you can go round regularly with one or more ready-cooked dishes and some fresh fruit, and take the baby out for a walk while mum gets some sleep. In order to coax her out for the fresh air and exercise she needs, you might telephone and ask her to put the baby in the sling and meet up for lunch at a local café, or, better still, tip off a friend of her own age to invite her.

Low self-esteem due to not getting her figure back as quickly as she hoped can contribute to the depression. An outing to shop for clothes will help. The clothes she needs are some that actually fit her as she is now, not as she was while pregnant or as she hopes to be again. Arrange to look after the baby while she goes to the hairdresser. Don't worry that your bossiness will annoy her or her partner – it probably will, but if it has the desired effect, it is worthwhile. And don't forget to reassure her that what she is feeling is perfectly normal and will not last.

MUMS SAY:
We always had a good relationship but my mother and

I have become even closer since I became a mother myself – she was a rock to me when I suffered severe PND after my son was born. I don't think I could have got through it without her.

I had post-natal depression and I cried on the phone to my mum for half an hour about how terrible I felt. When I stopped, hoping she would comfort me, all she said was, 'Poor Robert [my husband], fancy having to put up with all of that when he comes home from work.'

My in-laws saved my sanity when being at home on maternity leave was driving me to depression. They looked after the baby for two afternoons a week so I could go back to work.

Very rarely, post-natal depression is so serious that the mother has to be in hospital for psychiatric treatment. If she does go into hospital, the chances are you will be very much needed to look after the baby. This happened to one grandmother who put her life on hold and cared for her daughter's baby, taking it to visit mum in the psychiatric ward every day. Her daughter's consultant assured her that this played a major part in her daughter's recovery.

You just don't get on

Traditionally, sons-in-law have got it in for their mothers-in-law. There are books and websites devoted to mother-in-law jokes, bristling with men's hostility towards or contempt for their wives' mothers. But this ritual hostility is rendered fairly harmless by its stereotypical, predictable nature. What is far more disturbing somehow is the dislike (in some cases 'hatred' would not be too strong a word) that some women feel for their mother-in-law.

There are no familiar well worn jokes to take the sting out of this relationship. At least one third of the women in my survey showed some hostility to their mothers-in-law, their descriptions varying from the mild 'somewhat batty' to the vitriolic 'nasty self-centred old cow who isn't happy unless she is making someone else miserable.'

MUMS SAY:
I like that my mum tries to respect what I want when looking after my daughter (give or take an occasional packet of sweets) while my mother-in-law just spoils her rotten and buys her loads of stuff.

My mother-in-law is a dreadful grandparent... She was disappointed I had a boy. Her first words when she

found out I was pregnant were, 'Well let's hope it's a girl!' She likes him when she sees him but there is hardly any contact as she is a horrible person and didn't want to be a grandparent in the first place.

My mother-in-law was opinionated and self-centred. She could only relate to her grandchildren if they conformed to her views and her pattern of life.

The complaining women are, of course, not *your* daughter-in-law or mine. They are someone else's. Nevertheless their comments are bitter to the point of loathing, and there must be a reason for them. Jealousy is often a contributory factor – they are both in love with the same man, after all, and both compete for the love of the same children.

Over the past 30 years or so, feminism has also affected women's attitudes, bringing two generations into conflict. Daughters-in-law (and daughters, too) who hold down difficult and demanding jobs become incensed when confronted with the older generation's attitude to issues such as who does the housework, and who irons the shirts. Grannies may think the mums are over-sensitive, with their antennae out questing for a suspect attitude. It is true that if they cannot find it, some young women are touchy enough to imagine it.

But when a mother-in-law offers to sew a button on her grandson's school coat, or to run a hoover over the living room carpet, she is just doing what comes naturally. She probably doesn't even feel she is doing her daughter-in-law a favour. In her daughter-in-law's eyes her mother-in-law is guilty twice over. First she is silently accusing her of being unable to hold down a job *and* look after her home and family. Secondly she is making the old-fashioned assumption that it should be the wife who sews on the buttons, cleans the house and cooks the supper. The daughter-in-law, of course, feels her partner should be sharing the housework and childcare equally with her – if only his mother had brought him up to do as much...

In spite of the risk that your efforts may be misinterpreted by oversensitive mums, though, it is still worth making constructive offers of help, or just quietly getting on with what you can see needs to be done. You may be in worse trouble if you don't!

Mums say:
When my partner's mother comes to see us she does nothing to help.

My mother never does anything with the children –

just wants to be in their vicinity.

I had a difficult relationship with my mother-in-law but did not restrict access to her grandson, partly because she was ill and partly because I remembered the great pleasure and love between myself and my own grandmother.

My mother-in-law is only interested in her son – the children and I are appendages.

I was outraged when my mother-in-law took my twelve-year-old shopping and she came back with her ears pierced.

The relationship doesn't *have* to be difficult. A happy granny writes, 'Both my daughters-in-law are perfect. I can't criticise them in any way.' One of the secrets of success is for both sides to be open and frank. 'Don't be afraid to set boundaries' a daughter-in-law advises, 'If you think you've done your bit for mankind and don't fancy doing the nappy thing again, just say so!'

If your daughter seems hostile towards her mother-in-law, or if you are a mother-in-law on the receiving end of hostility, make allowance for the mum's exhaustion and irritability and try to understand how she feels, and what is upsetting or annoying her. Think back to the days when you were a daughter-in-law. Perhaps you found your mother-in-law irritating too.

Or could it be that you have unwittingly been stirring the pot? Perhaps you subconsciously feel the need to assert your position as top granny and encourage your daughter to find fault with her partner's mother. Or, in the case of your daughter-in-law, perhaps you hope to usurp the top granny's position by turning her against her own mother. Don't ever be tempted to turn the two sides of the family into opposing teams; the happiness of your child and your grandchildren is at stake. Luckily, children, in their wisdom, seem to love all their grandparents unconditionally, and we must try and keep it that way.

You may be longing to remind your daughter-in-law that she will probably be someone's mother-in-law herself one day. Restrain the urge, put your grievances out of your mind, pretend nothing is wrong, and play the part of a mother-in-law who gets on really well with her daughter-in-law or son-in-law. If you play the part with enough conviction it might even begin to come true.

MUMS SAY:
I think when a woman has her first child she develops a very special bond with her own mum. It is hard for

the mother-in-law, as she will never have that. I would advise mothers-in-law to appreciate it is a tricky relationship with a daughter-in-law and try to be sensitive about it. For both grannies it is a big change in life having their first grandchild and something that will take time to adjust to.

My father's mother adored my mother and was very sad when she and my father parted.

My father's mother and my mother got on really well, both being quite private women and believing in the importance of good manners. In fact, my mother says that her co-granny was her best friend.

Separation and divorce

Eeper Weeper, chimney sweeper
Had a wife and couldn't keep her.
Had another, didn't love her,
Up the chimney he did shove her.

The rise in the rate of divorce and remarriage has serious implications for grandparents. In 1961, when many of today's grannies were starting their families, there were 27,200 divorces in the UK. By 2003 the number had multiplied by six, reaching 166,700. In 2000, more than half of marriages (53%) ended in divorce, a rate only exceeded by Russia (65%), Sweden (64%) and Finland (56%). But that does not show the whole picture, because 40% of babies are born to parents who are not married, and the rate of separation among unmarried couples is higher than the rate of divorce among married couples. Looked at together, these statistics indicate that, whereas families where the parents stayed together 'until death did them part' used to be the norm, the opposite is now the case.

It is desperately sad for grandparents when their son or daughter's marriage ends in divorce. Every case is different and there are very complicated emotions involved. For children living in an unhappy household, their relationship with their grandparents may be the most stable element in a shifting world, and it may fall to the grandparents to see the children safely though the crisis.

Children often feel it is somehow their fault when one of their parents leaves home for good, and they will be in dire need of the extra love and reassurance grandparents can give. They may need you to tell them that their parents both still love them whatever happens. It is not good for children to live in an atmosphere heavily laden with emotion, so take them out whenever you get the chance, and do whatever you can to make sure they simply have fun in the way they do when life is normal.

A MUM SAYS:
My parents were not a great help during my divorce. There was a lot of 'I told you so' but no positive help or discussion. They don't think much of my current husband either – I now realise no man would have been considered good enough. But none of this has affected their grandparenting – they are devoted grandparents, and enjoy the relationship enormously.

GRANNIES SAY:
Be there to talk and listen. Never say the other parent is bad or horrid – there is always a reason for this or that. Never take sides (even though in your own mind you do).

Everything is discussed too much in front of them – whittling away the age of innocence.

Further good advice to grandparents is, to keep all lines of communication open. Do not judge anyone and do or say nothing that might jeopardise your own chances of continuing to see your grandchildren. This may mean biting your tongue from time to time to stop it running away with you. For example, if your son or daughter is about to marry for the second time, resist the temptation to phone on the eve of the wedding to ask if he/she is sure they are making the right decision.

The children involved in today's kaleidoscopic relationships acquire extra sets of step-grandparents as well as stepmothers and stepfathers. If your daughter or son remarries, you may become a step-granny; do welcome the opportunity if you can. The situation requires tact. Your new step-grandchildren have been through the upheaval of a broken marriage. They may be hostile towards you and their behaviour may be disruptive. Make allowances for the emotional turmoil they have suffered and be sensitive to the unhappiness and jealousy you may cause if you ignore them. Include them on outings and visits if they will come, but if they reject your overtures, back off: you may be trying to force an unwanted relationship on them.

Just gently show that you are there for them as you would be for your 'real' grandchildren. You may never feel the same about the 'steps' as you do about the babies you held in your arms, but you can still, in time, have a loving, rewarding relationship with them.

Grannies say:
With two broken marriages, resulting in two single mums, both working, 'grandma' is the first port of call for childcare, errands and meals... I consider it an

imposition – not by my daughters but by a society that has made life so difficult to cope with without working to make ends meet. (Age Concern)

I treat their 'real' granny with the kiddest of kid gloves.

When it comes to step-grannying, a bit of humility clearly goes a long way. One wise and much-loved step-grandmother says: 'My one rule is that a woman coming into the world of other people's children must deal with the hard truth that she has no more status than that of an au pair – and probably a rather unwelcome au pair at that. She is lowly, the object of suspicion with no authority. That's where you start. If you can earn affection and respect from that point, you'll be OK. In fact more than OK. The relationship will be based on a more equal respect and is much, much less conflict-ridden than mother/daughter. If you make assumptions that you are owed something simply because you married their father/grandfather, you will inevitably become the wicked stepmother which is almost impossible to overcome and will deprive you of the infinite pleasures of grandchildren.'

She is a woman of great generosity of spirit, and of common sense. Until she married a grandfather she had no grandchildren of her own, so that to love and be loved by these children meant a great deal to her. Her step-daughter says, 'My children consider her as granny and she has been amazing to me and them. She loves and cares but does not dote in the way she would if they were her own – she can slip in and out of the role as she is a step-grandparent. But we adore her.'

Illness and bereavement

We are grannies in sickness and in health, and, as we grow older, it is increasingly likely to be *our* sickness, *their* health. How much should our grandchildren be exposed to our frailty? One granny writes, 'I think a grandmother growing old and infirm can worry young children. I think there is a time to shield them from too much old age.'

Another remembers, with feelings of guilt, how reluctant she was to visit her 'old, overweight' grand-mother in hospital. Now that average life expectancy has increased, our grandchildren may be grown-up before we are old and ill, and it is our great-grandchildren that we will worry about.

For grown-up grandchildren, involvement with grandparents at the end of their life can be a good experience. It is sad to say goodbye to someone you love, and distressing if they are in pain. But, when a grand-parent is near the completion of a full life-span, what their children and grandchildren are witnessing is part of a natural cycle. This was brought home to me in my own family when my two children were both able to put their new babies into my 87-year-old mother's arms three weeks before she died.

It can seem right and proper to grandchildren to care for their elderly grandparents.

GRANDCHILDREN SAY:

I looked after my nan – not living in but arranging her hospital visits, liaising with social services, etc. She was very poorly for the last 20 years of her life and it upset me to think how cruel life can be.

I had a very good relationship with my grandmother, and when I was 22, I volunteered to look after her when she was dying. I could never have done bed-baths and toilet stuff for my mother or for someone my own age, but with Grandma it was normal, right and prop-er. I felt it was a real honour and still do – we had such fun together in her last weeks, laughing like drains and behaving like a couple of schoolgirls. It was a good time, and I cherish the memory, even the comic-horror events, like falling off the commode – no joke when your granny is 6ft 2!

Grannies sometimes become seriously ill well before the onset of old age, and those who have had the experience, having wondered initially whether they did right to allow their grandchildren to see them at their worst, have no regrets. One says, 'I was bald as a coot after my chemo, and worried about how the grandchildren would react. I needn't have worried, we laughed and joked about it and they stroked my scalp. To know they accepted me just as I was, boosted my morale enormously.' Another granny was 'amazed and delighted by my two granddaughters' kindness when I was ill. Before and after my cancer operation they were so physically, tactilely loving that they gave me their nits.'

If one of your grandchildren's parents is ill, you may have to look after the children. It is best, with the agreement of the other parent, to explain frankly, but in simple terms, the illness and its symptoms, and to take the children when you visit. If you keep children away from someone they love who is ill, the illness is likely to seem far worse in their imagination than in reality.

The same, I think, goes for death. Most children are intrigued by death and curious about it. When our grandson Oscar was three, Magnus, our ancient golden retriever, who had suffered all kinds of torture at Oscar's hands with patient resignation, died. We told him

Magnus was very old and tired and his heart had stopped working, and he made no comment. Oscar lives on a farm and the death of chickens, pigs and sheep is, if not an everyday occurrence, a normal one. Nevertheless, three weeks later our telephone rang.

'Hallo?' I said.

It was Oscar. He offered no greeting or introduction, just: 'Your dog is dead' – a simple confirmation of fact, as if he had been pondering the question during the interval and finally reached a satisfactory understanding of it.

> [My grandmother's] great affection for me, and her intense care for my welfare, made me love her and gave me that feeling of safety that children need. I remember when I was about four or five years old lying awake thinking how dreadful it would be when my grandmother was dead. When she did in fact die, which was after I was married, I did not mind at all.
>
> Bertrand Russell, *Autobiography*, 1961

The death of a close family member is inevitably sad for everyone, and we must face the fact that the first time it happens in your grandchildren's life is likely to be when an elderly person dies, perhaps a grandparent. Perhaps you. If it is you, the problem of how to comfort your grandchildren will not be yours.

In other circumstances, you must be prepared to answer children's questions. Naturally you will talk to their parents about what they have said to the children and what line they would wish you to follow. There may be difficulty in agreeing how to handle the situation if they are religious and you are not, or vice versa. For example, they or you may disapprove of any hint that there is an after-life. This is a big issue, and even quite small disagreements can be blown up out of all proportion when everyone involved is in a highly emotional state. You just have to remember that, even if the funeral arrangements are your responsibility, the beliefs or non-beliefs of your grandchildren are the responsibility of their parents.

GRANDCHILDREN SAY:
I remember being told my granddad had 'gone to heaven'. I was seven. My parents didn't tell me or my sister until after the funeral as they didn't want to upset us... I was very upset (he was the person who taught me to swing all by myself and all that sort of thing) and particularly that they had not taken me to say goodbye (which is what I understood a funeral to be).

I remember visiting my grandma in hospital when I was six. I went with my father when she was very ill with cancer. He was distraught and I realised for the first time that my granny was someone's mother. And I think I understood that she was dying.

GRANNIES SAY:
When my husband died the youngest one, then five, said, 'Pity Granddad had to die, he was a nice chap, wasn't he?'

My eldest grandson was badly affected by his grandfather's death. The others all cried but he couldn't, so a lady from Cruse came to talk to him and was a great help.

Should small children attend funerals? Should they see dead relations to say goodbye? These are momentous and irreversible decisions. A generation ago it was considered more compassionate to spare children from the trauma of death. Now opinion seems to have swung towards encouraging children to face reality. If a child can *see* the person who has died, it may help them to understand the finality of death, and achieve what today is referred to as 'closure'.

There are examples that seem to support this view. I was told about a young boy, a generation ago, whose elder brother had died suddenly. The boy did not attend his brother's funeral because his parents wanted to spare him pain. But he was inwardly unable to accept that his brother was dead, and searched for him unceasingly, fantasising, every time he met a boy of the right age, that this might be his lost brother. Today a formal goodbye, and mourning openly, are recognised as therapeutic for children as well as adults.

Even very small children seem able to recognise that a person who has died no longer inhabits his body. A mother touchingly recalls her toddler being with her when she found her father's body. Together they had gone out to tell 'gan-gan', the child's grandfather, that his supper was ready. He was outside, working on the car, and they found he had had a heart attack and died. In the midst of her shock, the mother heard the little girl saying, 'Gan gan gone.'

A grandmother describes how her two granddaughters reacted, at the ages of eleven and eight, to the death of a much-loved aunt who died aged 32 from a brain tumour. 'They loved my daughter and saw her throughout her terrible illness. They also said goodbye after she died – I wasn't sure at the time if this was right – it was. Now they often visit the grave and 'talk' to her and say prayers. On Easter Day we went to 'her' church and the younger one was saying prayers to us all beside the grave. The Vicar came and said, "Shall I take over?" "No", my daughter said, and continued. He was left with his mouth open in amazement!'

The decision that the two girls should see their young aunt after she had died, to say goodbye, was taken by their parents. It is not a decision that grandparents should try to influence, and I'm sure all parents and grandparents would agree that it is not something that should be forced on a reluctant child, as it used to be a hundred years ago.

Miscarriage

Two generations ago, miscarriages were not usually treated as bereavements. One granny remembers as a child in the 1950s staying with an aunt during her summer holidays. It was a rainy day and they were making a chocolate cake. They put the cake in the oven and her aunt said, 'I've just got to go upstairs for a bit. Make sure you check the cake in 20 minutes.' Her aunt returned in time to help her niece ice the cake, and shortly afterwards the doctor called. When she was older, the niece discovered what had happened that day. Her aunt had just popped upstairs to have a miscarriage. The idea, when miscarriages and stillbirths happened more frequently than they do now, was that you should take it in your stride and get on with your life.

Today there is a better understanding of just how distressing the loss of an unborn child is, and that it is natural and desirable for the parents to grieve for the baby, and for those around them to show compassion.

A MUM SAYS:
When my first pregnancy ended in an early miscarriage I was truly encouraged by my mother sharing with me her experience of early miscarriage and my mother in law telling me about her daughter's experience also. Finding out that it happened quite often really helped.

When a child dies

The death of your child is the worst thing that can happen to anybody, and far wiser counsel is available elsewhere than I could ever offer. If a grandchild dies, your main concern, even in the midst of your own distress, will be to comfort the parents. I would simply urge that you also make the dead child's siblings your special concern. The parents may be too distraught to help their other children, and it is easy for a sibling to feel that his own grief is only of secondary importance compared to theirs. A grandparent can help him talk about his feelings, and console him.

If it is your *own* son or daughter who dies, the parent of your grandchildren, then the need for you to be strong in the face of your own grief is even greater. This advice comes from a granny whose daughter died of cancer, leaving two young children: 'Keep the memory of the dead parent alive in a natural and relaxed way. Celebrate their life rather than grieving over their death. Always be ready to answer questions truthfully.' Another granny says, 'My son died when his daughter was three, and I and her mother saw her through this – we became very close.'

Sometimes, rather than adults helping children through the crisis of bereavement, it happens the other way around. A paediatrician who sees many families in the course of her work, and also has her own grandmother living with her, says, 'I hear stories about how grandchildren or great-grandchildren have helped grandparents get over bereavement. My grandmother is on her own now and has come to live with us. She loves the sound of tiny feet stomping over her head. It makes her think of the future instead of dwelling on the past, and she says that every day she gives thanks that she is so lucky.'

Where to get advice

Cruse Bereavement Care:
Day by Day Helpline 0870 167 1677
Website: www.crusebereavementcare.org.uk
Email: helpline@crusebereavementcare.org.uk

The Miscarriage Association:
Helpline 01924 200799
Website www.miscarriageassociation.org.uk
Email info@miscarriageassociation.org.uk

Child Death Helpline:
Freephone 0800 282986
Website www.childdeathhelpline.org.uk

For advice on gaining access to your grandchildren if it has been denied to you or may be denied, for example because of separation or divorce, or if the children are taken into care. And for advice about other problems grandparents may encounter:

The Grandparents' Association:
Advice line 01279 444964
Website www.grandparents-association.co.uk
Email info@grandparents-association.org.uk

Childhood songs and rhymes

Lullabies

Hush a bye baby on the tree top,
When the wind blows the cradle
will rock,
When the bough breaks the cradle will
fall,
Down will come baby, cradle and all.

***

Bye baby bunting,
Daddy's gone a-hunting.
Gone to fetch a rabbit skin
To wrap the baby bunting in.

***

Hush, little baby, don't say a word
Mama's gonna buy you a mockin' bird.
If that mockin' bird don't sing
Mama's gonna buy you a diamond ring.
If that diamond ring turns brass,
Mama's gonna buy you a looking glass.
If that looking glass gets broke
Mama's gonna buy you a billy goat.
If that billy goat don't pull,
Mama's gonna buy you a cart and mule.
If that cart and mule turn over
Mama's gonna buy you a dog named
Rover.
If that dog named Rover won't bark
Mama's gonna buy you a horse and cart.
If that horse and cart fall down,
Then you'll be the sweetest little baby in
town.

Action rhymes
(move the baby's legs up and down to
imitate marching)

Oh the grand old duke of York
He had ten thousand men.
He marched them up to the top of the hill
And he marched them down again.

And when they were up they were up
And when they were down they were
down
And when they were only halfway up
They were neither up nor down

***

Round and round the garden,
Like a teddy bear.
One step, two step,
Tickle him under there.

***

Incy wincy spider climbing up the
spout.
Down came the rain and washed the
spider out.
Out came the sunshine and dried up all
the rain.
Incy wincy spider climbed up the spout
again.

***

Two little dickie birds
Sitting on a wall,
One named Peter, the other named Paul.
Fly away Peter, fly away Paul.
Come back Peter, come back Paul.

***

Here we go round the mulberry bush,
The mulberry bush, the mulberry bush.
Here we go round the mulberry bush
On a cold and frosty morning.

This is the way we wash our hands,
[Brush our hair/clean our teeth/go to school]
Wash our hands, wash our hands,
This is the way we wash our hands
On a cold and frosty morning.

Counting rhymes

One two three four five,
Once I caught a fish alive
Six seven eight nine ten
Then I let it go again.

Why did you let it go?
Because it bit my finger so.
Which finger did it bite?
The little finger on the right.

***

One two, buckle my shoe.
Three four, knock at the door.
Five six, pick up sticks.
Seven eight, lay them straight.

Nine ten, a big fat hen
Eleven twelve, dig and delve
Thirteen fourteen, maids a-courting
Fifteen sixteen, maids in the kitchen.
Seventeen eighteen, maids in waiting.
Nineteen twenty, my plate's empty.

***

Ten green bottles hanging on the wall,
Ten green bottles hanging on the wall,
And if one green bottle should accidentally fall
There'd be nine green bottles hanging on the wall.

Nine green bottles hanging on the wall
etc etc

Knee ride rhymes

This is the way the children ride:
walk, walk, walk.
This is the way the ladies ride: trit-trot, trit-trot, trit-trot.
This is the way the gentlemen ride: canter-y, canter-y, canter-y.
This the way the farmers ride: gallop-y, gallop-y, gallop-y, gallop-y -
All fall down in the mud!

***

Row, row, row the boat
Gently down the stream,
Merrily, merrily, merrily, merrily,
Life is but a dream.

A farmer went riding upon his grey mare,
Lumpety bumpety bump,
With his daughter behind him so rosy and fair,
Lumpety bumpety bump.
The raven cried 'Croak' and they all tumbled down,
Lumpety bumpety, bump.
The mare broke her knees and the farmer his crown,
Lumpety bumpety bump.

Clapping rhymes

Pat-a-cake, pat-a-cake baker's man,
Bake me a cake as fast as you can.
Prick it and pat it and mark it with [child's initial]
And put it in the oven for [child's name] and me.

Others

This is the House that Jack Built...
This is the farmer sowing the corn
That fed the cock that crowed in the morn
That woke the priest all shaven and shorn
That married the man all tattered and torn
That kissed the maiden all forlorn
That milked the cow with the crumpled horn
That tossed the dog that worried the cat that chased the rat that ate the malt that lay in the house that Jack built.

New since our day

The wheels on the bus go round and round,
Round and round, round and round.
The wheels on the bus go round and round
All day long.
The wipers on the bus go swish, swish, swish,
Swish, swish, swish, swish, swish, swish.
The wipers on the bus go swish, swish, swish,
All day long.
The horn on the bus goes beep, beep, beep...etc

The people on the bus go chatter, chatter, chatter... etc

The baby on the bus goes wah, wah, wah... etc.

The bell on the bus goes ding, ding, ding... etc

***

Wind, wind, wind the bobbin up,
Wind, wind, wind the bobbin up.
Pull, pull; clap, clap, clap.
Point to the window,
Point to the door,
Point to the ceiling,
Point to the floor.
Clap your hands together, one two three,
Put your hands upon your knee.

Books

*Old favourites – more for your sake than the child's,
to keep the tradition going*

A book of nursery rhymes
Anything by Beatrix Potter
The Babar books
The Jungle Book
Little Black Sambo
Wind in the Willows
Winnie the Pooh

Modern classics

Bear Hunt
Bob the Builder
The Gruffalo
Hairy McClary
The Hungry Caterpillar
Owl Babies
Postman Pat
Thomas the Tank Engine
Where the Wild Things Are

Index

Acknowledgements

Many grandmothers and mothers and even some great-grandmothers gave up their time to answer my questions about their relationships. Some of the questions were intrusive, but the answers were always thoughtful and frank, sometimes funny and sometimes very moving. I would dearly love to thank each of them by name, but anonymity was part of the deal. So all I can do is offer whole-hearted thanks to my friends and relations and to the many people I met through www.mumsnet.com – a wonderful website for grandparents as well as for mums. My family need not be anonymous, and are at the core of the book, so thank you Sophy and Nick and Hugh and Marie; thank you from Granny Jane to Chloe, Max, Oscar, Guy and Freddie (in age order); and thank you Grandpa Rob.

I would like to thank the following for permission to use copyright material: Great Ormond Street Hospital Children's Charity for an extract from *Peter Pan* by J.M. Barrie; David Higham Associates for an extract from *Charlie and the Great Glass Elevator* by Roald Dahl; the Literary Trustees of Walter de la Mare and the Society of Authors as their representative for *The Cupboard*; the Society of Authors as the Literary Representative of the Estate of Alfred Noyes for an extract from *The Barrel Organ*; Frederick Warne & Co. for extracts from *The Tale of Peter Rabbit*, *The Tale of Mr Jeremy Fisher* and *The Tale of Johnny Town-Mouse* by Beatrix Potter.

For more on all aspects of modern grandparenting visit
Jane's website at **www.goodgranny.com**